BEVERLY GOLDBERG

The Free Press

NEW YORK LONDON SYDNEY SINGAPORE

AGE
WORKS

What Corporate America Must Do to Survive the Graying of the Workforce

THE FREE PRESS
A Division of Simon & Schuster Inc.
1230 Avenue of the Americas
New York, NY 10020

Designed by Deirdre C. Amthor

Manufactured in the United States of America

10   9   8   7   6   5   4   3   2   1

Library of Congress Cataloging-in-Publication Data

Goldberg, Beverly.
    Age works : what corporate America must do to survive the graying of
the workforce / Beverly Goldberg.
        p. cm.
    Includes bibliographical references and index.
        1. Aged—Employment—United States—Forecasting. 2. Downsizing of
organizations—United States—Forecasting. 3. Technological unemployment—
United States—Forecasting. 4. Displaced workers—United States—Forecasting.
5. Aged—United States—Economic conditions—Forecasting. I. Title.

    HD6280.G65 2000
    331.3'98—dc21
                                                                            99-055500

ISBN 0–684–85759–6

Also by Beverly Goldberg

Overcoming High-Tech Anxiety:
Thriving in a Wired World

Corporation on a Tightrope:
Balancing Leadership, Governance, and
Technology in an Age of Complexity

Dynamic Planning:
The Art of Managing Beyond Tomorrow

For Meg and Seth

Contents

Contents

List of Figures and Tables

List of Figures and Tables

Preface

For the past dozen years, I have spent my time in two very different worlds. After almost two decades at The Century Foundation, formerly the Twentieth Century Fund, a think tank devoted to research and timely analyses of economic policy and domestic issues, I added consulting to my work life. The corporate world I entered in the late 1980s was one of great and painful change, and my role as a consultant was to help companies discover what kinds of changes they had to make to survive and then to work with their employees to bring about those changes.

As the years went by, I kept waiting for the world of work to settle down, for a new set of rules of employment to be developed and a new set of relationships between employees and employers to emerge. After all, as the 1990s were drawing to a close, the economy was on such a long upswing without inflation that economists were wondering if a sea change had taken place that required rethinking the prevailing economic assumptions on which so many policy decisions were based. Unemployment was at a twenty-seven-year low. Stocks had risen to unimaginable heights. Economic growth was up, productivity finally seemed to have increased in the service sector, and consumer confidence seemed unshakable.

Despite all these economic triumphs, the wounds suffered by individual workers kept being reopened. Companies continued to believe that mergers and acquisitions were a path to increased profitability and every announcement of layoffs in the wake of those deals continued to grab headlines. The development of ever-newer technologies, making skills and often jobs obsolete, continued unabated. Most of those forced out eventually found new jobs, but they often did not pay as well as the jobs they'd lost. Uncertainty, with all its psychological discomforts, had become the new norm.

As a result, people now think about work very differently from the way they did in the 1950s and 1960s. Today, the paternal cultures that marked the large manufacturing and insurance companies and the strong unions of that period seem to have gone the way of the dinosaurs. Today, workers are personally responsible for remaining employable, for finding the time and money to go back to school to learn the new skills they need just to keep up with the demands of their industries or even to obtain the advanced degrees that will allow them to get ahead. Fear of losing their jobs keeps people working ever-longer hours to try to hold on. These fears also keep employees from pushing for the wage increases that were once normal in tight labor markets. The world of work is a world of anxiety and distrust.

A good example of how disillusioned we have become is our reaction when the leader of a company shows that he really cares about and feels a sense of responsibility toward the people who work for him. The media seize the story, the public demands more information, and the man of conscience becomes an instant folk hero, standing almost alone as an example of what is still right with the world of business. The story that comes to mind is that of Aaron Feuerstein, the owner of Malden Mills in Lawrence, Massachusetts. When a fire destroyed the plant Feuerstein owned, in December 1995, he announced within days that he would rebuild, that his employees would be paid their full salaries for thirty days, and that although the new plant would be modernized, workers would not be displaced—those who would need retraining to work with the new equipment would get it.

This seventy-year-old businessman became a national hero for not taking the insurance money and retiring, for not moving his plant to a place where labor was cheaper, for noting that loyal employees produced better-quality goods, thus creating loyal customers. What he did was right and good. The way it was celebrated, however, revealed our desperate need for some indication that the world of work we had idealized for so many years still was out there—somewhere. The amount of attention given this one example made clear how much Americans craved proof that the ideal world they so missed had not disappeared.

Unfortunately, one example of a good action, no matter how often referred to, will not change the new realities of the world of work today. Every time I walk into a corporation to conduct interviews, I encounter yet another tale of the effects of these never-ending changes:

- There is the fifty-year-old benefits manager at a major oil company who visibly shudders when the announcement is made that a new human resources system has just been adopted. Later she tells me that she's worn out, tired of trying to do her job in an environment marked by constant stress and the need to learn another new application every few months. She explains that she and her husband plan to retire "early, real early. . . . We've had it with what goes on. We'll find a way to get out, we'll do some teaching, maybe work part-time for a small company. Money isn't everything."
- There is the forty-six-year-old financial officer of a teaching hospital in the Midwest, the father of two teenagers, who refuses to have e-mail or a fax machine at home. "I've been downsized out of two hospitals already. This time, I'm not going to give up what's left of my home life to a job that will just

disappear. They want me to do these things so I can be reached anytime, day or night. If I lose my job over this, I'm going to try going into business for myself."

- There is the fifty-four-year-old member of a major consulting firm who says he's so tired of the long hours, of being passed over for interesting assignments by team leaders who are twenty years younger than he is, that he spends as much office time as he can investing in the stock market to build enough of a portfolio to feel comfortable retiring. Then he says, "I'll become a day trader. Or if worse comes to worse and that doesn't work, I'll pick up some short-term assignments. With my kids established, and my ex-wife remarried, I can live simply if I have to."

This drive to escape seems to permeate the corporate world. The desperation of these people is often reflected in their lack of awareness of how long a retirement they might have to support if they did leave. I was particularly aware of that issue because of my work at The Century Foundation, where one of the major issues we were examining was the future of the nation's Social Security system. The growing concerns about the future solvency of that program had caught the foundation's attention. The numbers were troubling. The huge demographic bulge known as the baby boomers was moving toward retirement age, and the generation that would replace the boomers was far smaller. Could the Social Security system survive? What would it take to support all these retirees in the next century? As we began to explore the numbers, we started looking at the whole issue of aging.

The combination of these issues presents a number of questions about how the aging of the baby boomers will affect business. What will the desire of the boomers to escape work in large corporations and the smaller size of the next generation of workers mean for corporate America? How early will today's workers retire? Is the dissatisfaction with corporations limited to the boomers? In the new world of work, the education and skills of the workforce are critical success factors because so many corporations are engaged in knowledge work. Who is responsible for seeing to it that workers have the skills that business needs? How will those with the requisite skills feel about work? Where will they choose to work?

I wrote this book to try to answer these questions in a way that would be helpful to all those who will be confronting the combination of problems created by the graying of the workforce and the changing attitudes toward the workplace.

Acknowledgments

This book grew out of three conversations.

First, at a luncheon roundtable discussion at The Century Foundation featuring Dr. Robert Butler, Pulitzer prizewinning gerontologist, Richard C. Leone, president of The Century Foundation, slipped me a piece of paper on which he'd written the words "The Business of Aging." When we spoke about his note later, we agreed it was a wonderful subject for a book, but I wasn't ready to think about writing another book at that time. I'd already coauthored two books exploring the kinds of changes that were necessary to build organizations that would thrive in the supercompetitive, increasingly global, technology-driven environment that marked the last decade of the twentieth century and was in the process of completing another book, this time examining how workers could cope with the demands of these technologies. I saved the note, however, taping it to the frame around my computer screen.

Second, a couple of months later, I was having a discussion with Sally Heinemann, the editorial director of *Bridge News,* who is in charge of the opinion pieces that *Bridge* runs online and supplies to newspapers throughout the country, about what policy issues were "hot." I've written many op-ed pieces for her, and in the course of talking about what I might write about next, I mentioned the words on that note. She suggested that I write a piece about the aging of the workforce. "The Graying of the American Workforce" appeared a week later.

Third, in the course of a conversation with Paula Duffy, the publisher of The Free Press, I mentioned the op-ed and my surprise at the number of papers across the country that had run the piece. She asked me to send her a copy. The next thing I knew, I was committed to writing this book.

These three people started me on the journey and provided enormous support throughout. I am grateful to all of them.

Although writing is a solitary occupation, research and interviews and peer review and revision are not. As a result, the list of people to whom I owe a great debt for the help they provided is long. Paul Golob, senior editor at The Free Press, served as counsel and guide throughout and his insights were invaluable. Tom Brown of Management General introduced me to many people who agreed to be interviewed, and he has read and commented on many drafts of the manuscript. Frank K. Sonnenberg of Sonnenberg, Haviland & Partners also provided valuable assistance and encouragement.

In addition, I have benefited greatly from my involvement with the work in which The Century Foundation has been engaged on the economy, aging, and the nature of work, particularly the study of the growth of service-sector employment by Stephen Herzenberg and John Alic; examinations of the relationship of the current world of work and the growing inequality in income and wealth in the United States by Paul Osterman of MIT, Edward Wolff of New York University, and James Galbraith of the University of Texas; and Dr. Butler's project involving a group of experts on various aspects of aging whose work the foundation published in *Life in an Aging America*.

The manuscript has had many readers and advisers, especially Richard C. Leone, Sarah Ritchie, Jason Renker, Greg Anrig, and Bernard Wasow of The Century Foundation; Wendy Mercer of the

Acknowledgments

Manhattan School of Music; Betsy Feist of Betsy Feist Resources and the National Writers Union; Sandra Winicur of Indiana University; Donna Zimmer of Shell Services International; and Eleanor Goddu of Ernst & Young. Daniel Melleby provided valuable research assistance. Sarah Nelson proofread the final version, and Tina King prepared the index. The book also has benefited from a careful editing by Meg Janifer, who never pulls her punches. And Rashida Valvassori once again provided assistance of all kinds at every stage of the process.

I owe an enormous debt to the people I have met not only in the course of the interviews for this book but those I have talked to in corporate America over the past dozen years while working on assignments for Siberg Associates. So many have been open about their feelings and told me of their fears and unhappiness about the changes they were facing. Often disillusioned by the actions of organizations they once believed in, they were determined to "keep up" despite enormous challenges and to do a good job for the company they worked for—for as long as they were working. I want to thank them all for being so open about their feelings.

I also thank my family for enduring my absorption in yet another book, especially my mother, Bessie Goldberg, who in her late eighties is still working three days a week as a volunteer. About a dozen years ago, she turned down a job offer that came as a result of her volunteer work because she did not want to "*have* to be there." We have had many discussions about this book, and she introduced me to some of the people I interviewed—active, involved senior citizens who contribute many hours of their time to others. She and her friends in service are my proof that age works.

AGE
WORKS

Introduction

America is facing a critical shortage of workers, especially skilled workers. In March 1999, unemployment in the United States fell to 4.2 percent. In Massachusetts, it was 3.3 percent; in Nebraska, 2.2 percent. It remained higher in states with very large cities—areas with large immigrant populations, high welfare rates, and poorly performing school districts where many citizens of working age do not have the skills needed to do the jobs that are available—and in some rural areas, such as Appalachia, where few industries are located.

Today, our economy can best be described as a knowledge economy, one in which education and skills matter more than ever before. This emphasis on skills is evident when the unemployment rate is broken down by educational level. In March 1999, unemployment among those without a high school diploma was 6.1 percent; high school graduates with no additional training had an unemployment rate of 3.4 percent; 2.8 percent of those with some college in addition to a high school diploma were unemployed; but only 1.9 percent of those with college degrees were unemployed.[1]

The shortage of workers, particularly skilled workers, cannot be ignored. As long as the economy remains strong, the current worker drought will continue. Moreover, if the demand for America's goods and services were to increase, many companies would be hard-pressed to take advantage of the situation. On the other hand, if the economy weakens, the situation will ease—but it will be only a temporary reprieve. The problem of finding enough workers to ensure corporate success and a strong economy will strike with unprecedented force in the second decade of this new millennium when the baby boomers, the seventy-six million people born between the close of World War II and 1964, begin to retire. The most problematic possibility is a continued strong economy that collides with the retirement of the baby boomers. That scenario would mean an economic catastrophe.

The generation that will replace the boomers, born between 1965 and 1983, is smaller, numbering only sixty-six million. What may make the problem even worse is that so many Americans are choosing not to wait until they reach sixty-five to retire: 60 percent of workers currently retire at sixty-two—a pattern that shows little sign of changing.

The painful fact is that labor force participation by those over fifty-five will have to increase by about 25 percent to maintain a constant total employment-to-population ratio from 2005 onward.[2] This means that corporations will have to do something to attract and retain millions of older workers if they are to survive this demographic shock wave.

The greatest obstacle facing corporate America when it comes to retaining workers is the anger and frustration that so many people feel toward the world of work today, especially toward large corporations. The road these corporations took to survive in a globalized, highly competitive, technologically advanced world is paved with the shattered hopes and dreams of those caught in the corporate restructurings that began in the late 1980s. Those who were "downsized" often took months if not years to find new jobs, frequently at lower pay, and they want to leave the workforce as soon as possible. So do those working ever-longer hours to do their jobs in lean organizations. And so do those who, simply to survive, took jobs that do not offer opportunities for advancement or demand anything in the way of initiative or creative input—a far cry from their initial expectations.

Younger workers do not provide a solution to the problem, for they have taken to heart the lesson that there is no such thing as corporate loyalty in return for sacrifice. These younger workers do not find working for large corporations attractive. They much prefer working for smaller companies, or better yet, working independently. Even if the younger generation were attracted to large companies, there still would be too few of them to fill all the available positions. Thus, corporate America will be forced to create a work environment that will turn a graying, disillusioned workforce into eager workers.

This challenge is enormous. Between 1970 and 1990, workforce participation among those over fifty-five fell by nearly 20 percent, costing the American economy roughly 2.6 percent per year of the gross national product.[3] If participation rates do not rise in the coming decades, the consequences could be even more severe. Averting that danger will require expenditures in the name of fairness, in essence the creation of a new social contract between employers and employees. Organizations that seek to survive and prosper will have to learn to think out-of-the-box to win the coming competition for workers.

The Day of Reckoning Is Approaching

Given the tight labor market as the twentieth century drew to a close, the talk around the water coolers in offices across America should have changed dramatically. Instead of the sad comments so common in the midst of the huge downsizings of the late 1980s and early 1990s about, for example, "Poor Joe from accounting— three months and he hasn't even been called for an interview," the comments should have changed to "We can't find anyone to fill that job in accounting."

That is not the way it happened. Joe's old job simply disappeared. Business process reengineering and technology eliminated the need for most of the people with Joe's skills. Now, the talk around the water cooler is both "Poor Joe from purchasing—three months and he hasn't even been called for an interview" and "How are we ever going to find someone with experience with that design application who can also manage a team?"

The economic growth and prosperity of the late 1990s resulted in the lowest unemployment rates in a quarter of a century, and when it came to literate, skilled employees, the numbers dropped even more. In Silicon Valley in 1999, finding skilled workers was so difficult that the major companies in the area appealed to Congress for the second year in a row to open America's doors to more foreigners with technology skills; they argued that it was the only way to make up a shortfall of more than 150,000 jobs requiring such advanced skills.

At the same time that unemployment was reaching these new lows, Joe and hundreds of thousands like him couldn't find jobs that matched their training and skills. They dropped out of the labor market or settled for less skilled work just to pay the rent. And while employers were complaining about how hard it was to find employees, corporations were continuing to announce ever more massive layoffs. In the first four months of 1998, planned layoffs hit a ten-year high of almost 188,000; for the first four months of 1999, 264,920 planned layoffs were announced—and the trend shows no sign of abating.[4]

This churning is not a reflection of capriciousness on the part of companies. They are engaged in a battle for a competitive edge in a difficult global environment. However, the more profitable a company is, the more its stockholders and CEO are the only big winners, the more the resentment grows. It does not matter that many of these layoffs are the result of companies reducing staff size as they combine various departments in the course of mergers and acquisitions (a revival of the mergers and acquisitions fever of the 1980s). Or that they are the result of companies turning to new, more efficient methods of production that require fewer people and people with different, usually new, skills. Or that new jobs are being created in smaller companies set up to handle the work these large organizations decide to outsource because doing so is less expensive.

The problem lies in the fact that the losers so often seem to be the loyal, caring employees who thought their lives were on a comfortable track. They believed there was an implicit social contract in place whereby the companies to which they had devoted their working lives would return that loyalty with employment. But Joe wasn't offered training for one of the new jobs that opened up a few months after he left.

Many downsized employees find work with start-ups, but these firms pay far less than large corporations and rarely provide benefits. Others find themselves back at their old companies as "independent contractors," earning less than before and with no benefits. Some, downsized for the second or third time, simply drop out of the labor market and attempt to make it through to retirement on savings or a spouse's earnings or try to set up a small business to tide themselves over until they can collect a pension.

The real reason that "poor Joe from accounting"—or from purchasing or from a variety of other positions—doesn't find a new job even though companies are desperate for workers is the constant adoption of ever-newer technologies. It is easier to find young people with the skills to use the new technologies that now produce the results Joe did than to retrain Joe; not only does this save retraining costs, but these new entry-level workers do not earn as much as workers who have acquired seniority.

These developments have had a costly result. Older workers are discouraged and disillusioned. Younger workers have heard the message that businesses, especially large corporations, do not care about workers. What will these organizations have to do to find and attract the workers they will so desperately need? Furthermore, how can they ensure that those workers will have the skills they need, when they need them?

Introduction

The current economic boom offers companies an opportunity to come to terms with the problem of creating a workforce that will fill their needs as the enormous baby-boom generation retires. Doing so requires more than developing programs aimed at helping integrate older workers into the workforce. The far smaller generation that follows the boomers does not share the feelings about work that nourished the growth of large corporations in the 1950s. Unlike their predecessors, they will work hard and learn what they must to do the best job possible, but they do not feel that the company they work for is owed the kind of loyalty and sacrifice that is owed to family. They realize that employability is the key to survival, so they choose work that offers training and growth—often with smaller companies—knowing they will move to a number of different companies in the course of their careers.

The crux of the problem is the combination of the boomers' retirement from the workforce and the kinds of work life preferred by the generation that will replace them, as well as the smaller size of that generation. Will corporate America recognize the problem in time to build the kind of workplace—one that provides employees with a work life that echoes the flexible organizational structures built by corporations over the past decade—that will be necessary to attract and retain enough workers to survive and even take advantage of opportunities for growth in the next decades?

Some companies affected by worker shortages in the tight labor markets of the late 1990s have begun to move in this direction. Some have been instituting worksharing arrangements and developing phased retirement programs. Others have been seeking new ways to retain or even recruit retired or retiring employees. For example, Whirlpool Corp. and GTE Corp. have hired retired workers to fill short-term assignments abroad rather than relocate younger workers who are hard to replace and who would resist the disruptions to their families caused by such months-long moves. Florida-based Home Shopping Network fills positions for its peak periods with seniors recruited from nearby retirement communities. McDonald's has developed programs designed to recruit seniors—and not just for jobs as hamburger flippers; it also has a managerial program aimed at seniors. The problem is that for every company finding new ways to recruit and retain the workers they need, there are far too many that have buried their heads in the sand.

Moreover, the major public and media focus on the baby boomers centers on what their aging means for the Social Security system, which provides most of the elderly with a good portion of their retirement incomes, rather than on the effects of the coming labor shortage on business. The problem in the context of Social Security is how the far smaller population of workers of the next several decades will be able to continue to support the Social Security system as the ratio of workers to retirees becomes ever smaller. The truth of the matter is that fixing the system is not a problem when the economy is strong. The problem is rather how to ensure that there will be enough workers to keep the economy strong when the boomers retire.

There are factors at work that may blunt the trend toward early retirement. First, there is the failure of Americans to save adequately for retirement, combined with their longer life spans. Estimates are that most boomers now in their forties and fifties have saved only a third of what they will need to supplement their Social Security in retirement. At the same time, the pensions that previous generations depended on for retirement have to a large extent disappeared, as has longtime service with a single company and union membership.

Add to this mixture the fact that older people are far healthier than those in comparable age groups a decade ago; today's sixty- to seventy-year-olds are as healthy as fifty-five- to sixty-five-year-olds were then. A growing number of seniors choose to retire to the snowbelt so they can ski in winter, and many seniors continue to volunteer long hours because they love what they do.

Older workers are also more employable than they used to be

because three-quarters of the jobs in this nation today are in the service sector rather than manufacturing, a shift as profound as the switch from farming to manufacturing a century ago. Service-sector and knowledge-based jobs are less physically demanding; they are more like academic positions and the law, fields where people work well into their seventies and even eighties.

Now look at the corporation today—an organization re-shaped and restructured in response to technological advances, increased competition, and globalization of the economy. Corporations pride themselves on having become learning organizations, flexible and responsive to market demands. They change what they do and how they do it whenever such change will provide them with a competitive advantage. In fact, it is this ability to change that has caused so much unhappiness among workers. Yet, flexible as they are in terms of their structure, these organizations have not figured out how to make a flexible workforce an integral part of the way they work. They are still mired in the old model of work when it comes to employees.

Creating a New Path

Future success will depend on the ability of employers to attract the best and brightest from the many different groups that comprise the workforce. Among those groups are "older" workers, and if employers take the time to study older workers instead of thinking of them as a last resort, they will discover that older workers are not a homogeneous group; they differ from one another enormously when it comes to abilities, desires, and needs. Some older workers are at a senior level and could serve their former employers well as consultants. Some could pass along experience and knowledge to younger workers. Others have skills no longer in demand but knowledge of the institution and how it works that would make them valuable in other jobs. Older workers are trainable: the explosion in the number of older people attending our nation's colleges and universities is evidence of that.

Depending on their needs, both financial and personal, these older employees might want to work part-time, full-time, sporadically, or not at all. Some have far more stamina than others. Some want to retire to do something other than what they have spent their working lives doing; for example, many who retire with adequate resources are determined to do something in their later years that they see as "giving back" to the world, "making a difference." Others are just tired of what they have been doing and hope retirement will provide "something new."

Turning to older workers as a solution for tight labor markets is made more difficult by the misperceptions so many have about them. For example, older employees are often considered resistant when it comes to instituting changes, adopting new technologies, and sparking innovation and creativity. Generational differences in values and beliefs also create misunderstandings. In the end, getting the most out of older workers requires finding new ways of managing. But it can be done—and done very successfully.

Over the next fifteen to twenty years, employers are going to have to deal with a workforce in which one out of five—and then one out of four—employees is going to be over fifty-five. Adding a group of still older workers to their numbers—those who would otherwise choose to retire early—will not make a major difference to the adjustments that will be needed simply because the population itself is aging. The size of the baby-boom generation and the media focus on it over the years has made that generation the face of America as it has moved through each stage of the life cycle—and that shows no sign of changing.

The question really is, What will it take to make the transition to an older workforce as fruitful as possible for older workers, corporate America, and society?

First, corporate leaders will have to accept that there is a real problem. Human resource professionals are becoming increasingly aware that the difficulties they are having with recruitment and retention because of current tight labor markets may not disappear. The major associations of human resource professionals have begun, as part of their long-term examinations of issues such as retirement planning and benefit packages, to point to demographic projections as a warning that recruitment and retention will remain the largest problem facing the profession for decades to come.

Corporate leadership does not seem ready to face this issue for a number of reasons. First, many of these leaders are themselves a part of an older generation and plan to retire soon themselves. For somewhat younger leaders, since it is an issue that will not affect their organizations for more than a decade—the official retirement age of the first of the boomers is 2011—they stand to gain more by focusing on more immediate problems, those that will affect profits in the short term. Others assume that the problem will be solved by technological advances, which will further increase productivity and efficiency, making possible ever-smaller workforces. After all, the lesson of the past decade has been that the work gets done and profits soar the more you downsize; someone picks up the slack, whether it is retained workers willing to put in ever-longer hours, outsourcers, contingent workers, or temps. Others just don't believe that older workers are valuable. Their prejudices are many—older workers hurt the corporate image, are slow to accept change, don't have the stamina or strength of younger workers, aren't as productive.

Second, those thinking about retiring early must be brought to face the realities of retirement. In particular, they need to understand that if they retire as early as they indicate they want to, they may spend two decades in retirement, which will have adverse effects on their ability to pay for the kind of retirement they now envision for themselves. They also need to examine the differences between retirement from hard physical labor to leisure and retiring from stimulating, creative work. How do they really want to spend the last quarter of their lives?

Introduction

Looking Ahead

The graying of America (and the rest of the world) seems statistically inevitable, and this reality will affect the economy and the workforce in numerous ways. The percentage of older people in the population is increasing dramatically and will continue to do so for decades as a result of the baby boom, increased life expectancy, and falling fertility rates. In 1790, the median age in America was 16; in 1890, it was 21; in 1990, it was 33; in 2040, it will be almost 39. These changes are reflected in the composition of the workforce. The median age of Americans in the workforce (which is higher than the median age of the overall population because of the number of nonworking youth) will reach 40 in 2005; in 1979, it was 34.7. Moreover, starting in 2011, when the first of the boomers start to retire, half of all prime-age workers will be over 45. The ways that business adjusts to this change will have an enormous impact on all our futures. The other important set of numbers involves retirement, including life expectancy rates, income expectations in retirement, and plans for retirement lifestyles.

Once the problem is clear, the solution becomes clear: Making changes that will convince older Americans to participate longer in the workforce. Doing that, however, will require developing a deep understanding of the forces that have been pushing people out of the workforce—the disillusion created by downsizing and displacement, the push toward retirement as a way of life that began in the 1950s and peaked in the 1970s, and the attitudes toward older workers that discourage continued effort, and even participation. With that understanding, and a study of successful efforts already under way in some corporations, we can begin to shape a new social contract that will encourage people once again to consider large corporations good places to work.

The most important group of workers when it comes to the near future are the baby boomers. When and how they choose to retire from work will determine what retirement looks like in the first half of the twenty-first century, and that will determine the size

11

of the available workforce. Indeed, the only certainty about the aging of the baby boomers is that it will shake the economy to its foundations if American businesses do not prepare for it. Predicting exactly what difference it will make is an uncertain art at best. Therefore, what firms need to do first is find ways to overcome the resentment they have created as they took action to increase their competitiveness in a globalized economy. Then they must put in place strategies and programs that can turn silver into gold.

Part I

The Problem

Part 1

The Problem

Chapter 1

Going by the Numbers

The demographics of the baby boom point to a future in which there will be a much older workforce—one that may be far too small to meet corporate America's needs. The problem is not simply too few people to replace the previous generation but also too many people leaving the workforce earlier than ever before and people increasingly unwilling to work ever-longer hours for large organizations.

Those opting out of the workforce often choose that path because they are tired of having to accept constant change and increasingly more difficult work conditions. They have been taught that retirement is a great good, and they no longer believe that business is interested in anything but the young and computer savvy. If all those over forty retire as early as they currently plan to, they will exacerbate a perilous demographic situation.

Some will doubtless respond that the solution is to gear up the great American propaganda machine. Surely the country that convinced women to enter the workforce during World War II and then leave it for hearth and home when the soldiers came marching back from war can convince baby boomers to keep working well past the current popular retirement age of sixty-two. Those who advocate this solution forget that Americans today are better educated and more knowledgeable than earlier generations. Baby boomers are extremely well versed in how advertising and propaganda work and have learned to be skeptical. Besides, in the age of the Internet, such propaganda is subject to quick exposure—and widespread derision.

Demography, moreover, is not destiny. Demographic projections are subject to any number of outside forces such as wars, radical changes in economic conditions, and enormous shifts in lifestyle. People are not numbers; they change in response to all kinds of social events as well as major forces. Analysts examining birthrates per woman from 1946 to 1960 had no idea that, with no war and no recession, they would plummet only five years later. In fact, demographers never expected the initial high birthrates of the immediate postwar period to continue for nineteen years.

In addition, the predictions on which most analyses of future population trends are based are intermediate projections. The U.S. Bureau of the Census offers three sets of assumptions—low, intermediate, and high. For example, life expectancy rates for males born in 2000 vary from 72.1 in the low-assumption series to 73.0 for the intermediate series to 73.7 under the high series. The spread of one and a half years between the low- and high-assumption sets seems minor until you think about how much extra that year and a half could cost in Social Security payments and how much additional income someone would have to save to supplement Social Security during that period.

Barring any of these changes, the industrialized nations will face a major problem in the first half of the twenty-first century: The shift in size between the baby-boom and baby-bust cohorts could have catastrophic effects on the world economy. The problem involves not just the aging of the workforce but the aging of the population as a whole. This phenomenon is likely to have major effects on the kinds of goods and services that will be in demand in the future and how they will be provided, as well as who will pay for what.

A Birth Bonanza

The economic gloom created by the Great Depression, the years of uncertainty about being dragged into another war, and World War II itself provoked a degree of caution about the future that was reflected in birthrates. In the period 1927–45, forty-nine million children were born in the United States. In the aftermath of World War II, the national elation over victory and the joy and exuberance at the return of our soldiers erased the mood of the 1930s and early 1940s. Life had been on hold for too long, and we were ready to meet all challenges. Some seventy-six million children, the baby boomers, were born in the nineteen years between 1946 and 1964 inclusive. In the following nineteen years (1965–83), the number fell to sixty-six million, a 13 percent shortfall.

The delay in births during the years leading up to the baby boom is clearly visible in the two bands in the 1960 pyramid in Figure 1.1 that represent those aged twenty to twenty-nine in that year. The three far larger bottom bands in the 1960 pyramid represent the first waves of the baby boom. (Until 1940, if ages were presented in this kind of figure, the result clearly resembled a pyramid—that is, the largest percentage of the population was the youngest, the smallest group was the oldest.) The 1990 pyramid in Figure 1.1 shows the full impact of the baby-boom generation.

The high birthrates that began as the war ended brought about the generation that, since its birth, has dominated every aspect of American life. More elementary schools were built in 1957 than in any year before or since, and the same happened with high

Figure 1.1 The Changing Shape of America's Age Profile, 1930–2020

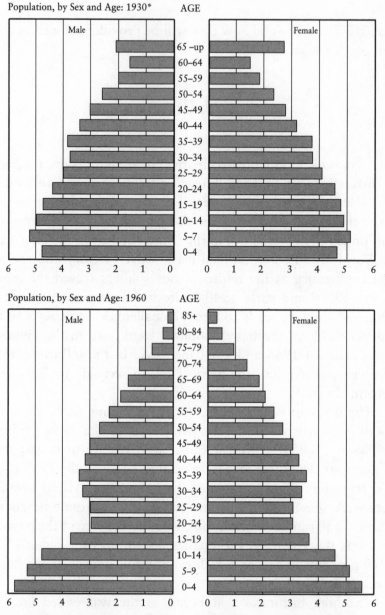

Population, by Sex and Age: 1930* AGE

Population, by Sex and Age: 1960 AGE

Source: Valerie Lawson, U.S. Bureau of the Census, Current Population Reports, various series (Washington, D.C.: Government Printing Office).

*The data for those over sixty-five is not broken down because so few were seventy and older in 1930.

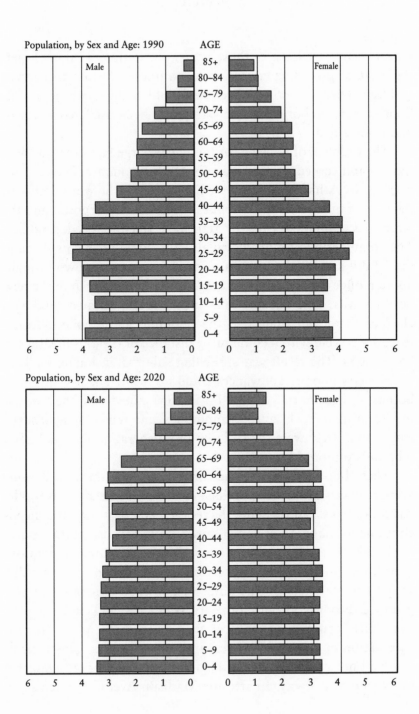

Population, by Sex and Age: 1990

AGE

Male

Female

85+
80–84
75–79
70–74
65–69
60–64
55–59
50–54
45–49
40–44
35–39
30–34
25–29
20–24
15–19
10–14
5–9
0–4

6 5 4 3 2 1 0   0 1 2 3 4 5 6

Population, by Sex and Age: 2020

AGE

Male

Female

85+
80–84
75–79
70–74
65–69
60–64
55–59
50–54
45–49
40–44
35–39
30–34
25–29
20–24
15–19
10–14
5–9
0–4

6 5 4 3 2 1 0   0 1 2 3 4 5 6

schools ten years later. In those years, our nation faced, and met, the costs of providing education to an unprecedented number of children. The United States became a child-centered nation as millions of children born after the war had to be housed, fed, clothed, and entertained.

The problem of housing for these new, large families was enormous—and turned out to be a spur to the economy. The nation's housing stock had not been replenished during the war because of the lack of manpower and supplies for domestic purposes, and the large new families started by returning veterans needed homes. The combination of money available for down payments through the GI Bill and the desire for a piece of land of one's own brought about a huge expansion in housing construction. Much of the new housing was built outside large urban areas, because land was cheaper there, but thanks to the booming automobile industry, these areas were within commuting distance of the jobs in large urban centers. The result was sprawling suburbs, including malls in which hefty boomer allowances could be spent. The first group of boomers (those born from 1946 to 1955) joined with the war babies to bring us rock 'n' roll, communes, and rebellion against the status quo. They were the children of a generation that had good jobs and comfortable incomes.

These boomers became the consumers that Madison Avenue grew to cherish for their purchasing power. Their styles were the nation's styles. And as they have aged, their wants and needs continue to shape American culture simply because of their numbers. Whatever they have wanted—from retaining a youthful appearance to a love for convertibles—has tended to have a disproportionate effect on the kinds of goods American businesses produce. From workout clothes to skin care, makeup, and hair dyes (now common for men as well as women), products that help maintain a youthful appearance are sure bets. This generation will not go gentle into old age but intends to rage against it every step of the way, an attitude Madison Avenue is once again responding to, as is evident from advertisements for everything from vitamins to real estate that feature mature but oh so attractive and hardy seniors crossing streams as they hike in well-tended woods.

The second group of boomers (born from 1956 to 1964) tends to get lost in the very large shadow of the first. This group includes the first of the "wired babies"—members of the computer generation that has been reshaping the world of work. In many ways, their experiences are more like those of the cohort that came after them. Demographically, however, they are treated as part of the boomer cohort.

The Graying of the Workforce

In the future, the business world will be dominated by a simple fact: The workforce will grow increasingly grayer (under all that hair dye) as aging boomers drive the median age of the population—and the workforce—higher. In late 1996, when the first of the baby boomers reached fifty, the Census Bureau announced that the number of those in their fifties would increase by 50 percent—by twelve million—from 1996 to 2006.

- In 1995, 11.8 percent of the population was between fifty-five and sixty-nine years of age; in 2020, 18.4 percent of the population will be between fifty-five and sixty-nine years of age. That's a growth in absolute numbers from 31 million to 59.4 million.
- In 1995, those in their prime working years (aged twenty to fifty-four) represented 50.3 percent of the population; they will represent only 43.9 percent of the population in 2020.

In 2011, the first of the baby boomers will turn sixty-five. By

Figure 1.2

Population 65 and Over, Selected Years, 1960–2030

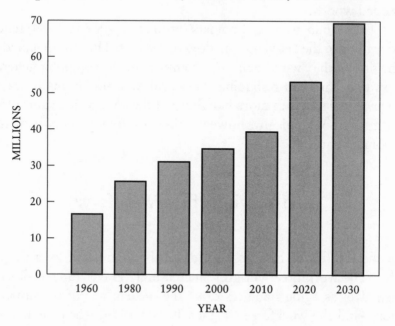

Source: U.S. Department of Commerce, Bureau of the Census, "Aging in the United States—Past, Present, and Future" (Washington, D.C.: Government Printing Office, July 1997).

2020, most boomers will be in their pre- and actual retirement years. The population aged sixty-five to seventy-four thus will grow by 74 percent between 1990 and 2020, while the population under sixty-five will grow by only 24 percent. The numbers are impressive: In 2030, there will be more than four times as many people in this country over the age of sixty-five as there were in 1960, and twice as many as there are today (see Figure 1.2).

Of course, the issue is not merely how many older people there

Figure 1.3

Changes in Labor Force Participation Rates, 1950–1995

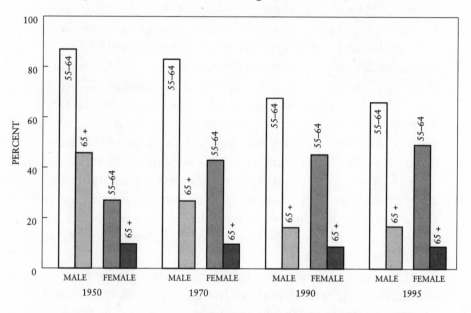

Source: U.S. Department of Commerce, Bureau of the Census, *Historical Statistics of the United States* (Washington, D.C.: Government Printing Office, 1975) and Bureau of Labor Statistics, Current Population Surveys, various years.

are but what they choose to do at any given age. In general, labor force participation rates of older workers have undergone a significant change over the past two decades. The overall rates have fallen steadily for all workers over sixty-five, but the rates for men between fifty-five and sixty-four, which remained over 80 percent during the 1950s and 1970s, dropped to 66 percent by 1995. On the other hand, labor force participation rates of women from fifty-five to sixty-four have risen steadily over the same period (see Figure 1.3).

23

The fall in participation rates for men over fifty-five is strongly related to the downsizings that took place during the late 1980s and early 1990s, a point that will be explored in greater detail in chapter 3. The increased rates for women since the 1970s are explained in part by the same events that caused men's rates to fall. (The sizable increase in women's participation from 1950 to 1970 was a result of the women's movement.) Many older women entered the labor force to help support their families as men lost their jobs then accepted lower-paid or temporary employment. Another contributing factor was the increase in divorce among couples who had trouble handling the psychological effects of downsizing; in all too many of those cases, the costs of extended unemployment meant that there was far less wealth and little income to share after the divorce, pushing former homemakers into the workforce. And for both sexes, the fall in participation rates for those sixty-five and older has more to do with the acceptance of retirement as a norm.

If this tendency of men to drop out of the workforce earlier continues, along with the relatively small increases in the number of women remaining, it will present quite a problem for American corporations. As the century neared its close, a booming economy brought tight labor markets. Part of the problem was that many in the fifty-five and older age brackets had spent so much time looking for work during the downsizings of the early 1990s that they simply dropped out. Because they believe that prejudice toward older workers has not lessened, many will not even attempt to return, and most certainly will not consider returning to full-time work after so many years in retirement. Another issue for many is that their skills, which were already in less demand when they left the workplace, are now totally outdated. Those who attempt to return may find that only a limited number of poorly paid, low-skilled jobs are available to them.

The perception of prejudice against older workers is not completely unfounded; data show that older workers continue to take longer to find new jobs than younger workers. Thus, while businesses may feel forced to accept older workers, most still do so grudgingly. The problem is that business still has not awakened to the fact that older workers are going to be the norm in the future, that they are healthier than their counterparts in earlier generations, and that with proper training older workers can learn as well as younger workers.

Muddying the Water: The Focus on the Elderly as Dependents

One of the major issues that needs to be examined because of its effects on retirement is life expectancy. Increased life expectancy indicates that people are healthier and so can work longer; it also means that people will spend a longer time in retirement, which must be taken into account when thinking about how much money will be needed to finance retirement. Unfortunately, however, most of the focus on increased life expectancy has come from those who predict a demographic disaster in the making as the ratio of workers to pensioners changes. Somehow, they seem to neglect the other side of the coin: the effects of lower fertility rates on total dependency ratios.

Increases in Life Expectancy

The average life expectancy of males and females born in 1945 is 61.4 years; for those born in 1965, the tail end of the baby boom, it is 70.3 years. The number of years differs for men and women; moreover, the number of years one is likely to live if one reaches 65 also is different (see Figure 1.4).

All this has an impact on the ratio of workers to pensioners. In

Figure 1.4

Life Expectancy at Birth and at Age 65, Selected Years, 1940–2020

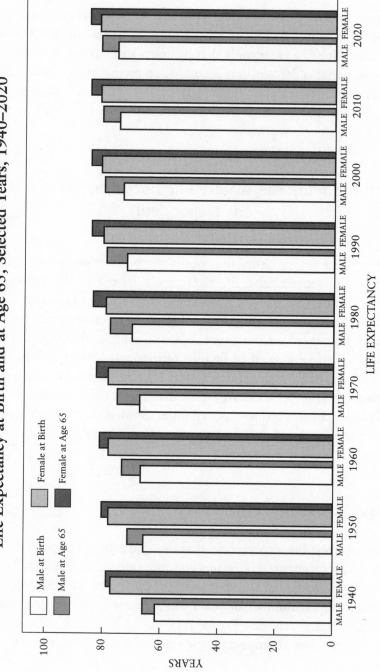

Source: U.S. House of Representatives, Committee on Ways and Means, *1998 Green Book* (Washington, D.C.: Government Printing Office, 1998), p. 22, Table 1–14.

determining future dependency ratios, it is important to take into account not only that a male baby boomer born in 1950 who reaches 65 will live another 12.8 years and a female 15.1 years, but also that early retirement increases the number of years spent in dependency.

Declines in Fertility Rates

The total dependency ratio, however, depends as well on fertility rates, which have declined since 1964 and show no signs of rising. Indeed, there are strong indications that they are on a continuing downward spiral worldwide. The U.N. *World Population Estimates and Projections: 1998 Revised Edition* indicates that in the industrial nations the average fertility rate is 1.42, far lower than the 2.1 rate that ensures population stability. In the United States, the fertility rate is hovering at 2.0, just below the number needed for replacement.[1]

This trend eliminates one possible solution to America's coming worker shortfall. Although children born now, at the turn of the century, could begin to expand the pool of available workers as early as 2018, people are unlikely to consider this a reason to have additional children. In fact, experience in other nations that have attempted to reverse this decline through, for example, tax credits for larger families indicates that fertility rates are likely to continue to fall here and throughout the world.

At the same time, the numbers of the "oldest old" (those over eighty-five) are increasing dramatically. In 2020, in the United States, there will be 6.5 million people over eighty-five, double the number in 1990. The combination of longer life and lower fertility changes the face of the population—and its needs. In 1998, Italy, with its 1.2 fertility rate, became the first nation with more people over the age of sixty than under the age of twenty. A number of other nations are also moving in this direction; it will take a bit longer for the United States because birthrates among immigrant populations remain somewhat higher than replacement rates for at least a generation after arrival. But we are moving in that direction.[2]

The Specter of Dependency

Although increasing longevity and declining birthrates change the face of the population, they do not necessarily affect total dependency ratios. In 1960, every one hundred people between the ages of eighteen and sixty-four had 65.3 dependents under eighteen and 16.9 over sixty-five; in 2030, when the baby boomers will have retired, every one hundred people between the ages of eighteen and sixty-four will have 43.1 dependents under eighteen and 35.7 over sixty-five (see Figure 1.5).

Doomsayers use the projected ratio of workers to pensioners to prove that the real issue when it comes to the aging of the population is the changing worker-to-pensioner ratio. Given that more than half of the oldest old, almost 1.5 million people, currently live in nursing homes, the nation does face a nursing home population that will double in the next thirty years. What these Cassandras manage to avoid when forecasting a disaster in the making is that in 1960 the total dependency ratio was higher than it will be in 2030, when the majority of boomers will have retired.

Somehow our nation managed to deal with having 82.2 dependents for every 100 workers in 1960. We built the schools and playgrounds needed for all these young dependents and found teachers to teach them. The dependency ratio of the future means that every 100 workers will be supporting 78.7 dependents in 2030. The questions this raises are: Will nursing homes be the growth industry of the future? If so, who will take on those jobs, which are generally low-paying, blue-collar positions? And who will pay for the costs of this care? These questions are not unlike

Figure 1.5

Number of Dependents per 100 Persons
Age 18 to 64 Years, 1940–2030

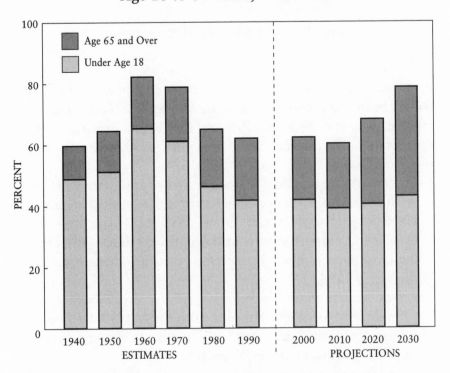

Source: Jennifer Cheeseman Day, *Population Projections of the United States by Age, Sex, Race, and Hispanic Origin: 1995 to 2050,* U.S. Bureau of the Census, Current Population Reports, P25-1130 (Washington, D.C.: Government Printing Office, 1996).

the questions asked in 1960 about how our nation would educate all those children.

The financial and labor force implications of the needs of the elderly must be addressed. But if we could find a way to build those schools, why should we assume we won't be able to build nursing homes? It is also important to keep in mind that people are healthier than ever before, and thus the age they retire may well change, further lessening the total dependency ratio.

The Drive to Early Retirement

If the tendency to choose early retirement continues, however, it will intensify the problem of ensuring an adequate workforce during the next few decades. The problem began in earnest two decades ago, when the push to get people to retire began:

- In 1950, 45.8 percent of all men sixty-five and older were still in the workforce; that number dropped to 16.8 percent by 1995.
- In 1970, 83 percent of men aged fifty-five to sixty-four were in the labor force; only 66 percent of men in that age bracket worked in 1995.

The Employee Benefit Research Institute's 1997 Retirement Confidence Survey indicates that the trend toward early retirement is likely to continue (see Table 1.1).

In addition, as Table 1.1 makes clear, the drive to retirement increases as age decreases; that is, more younger people plan to retire early than older people. While only 7 percent of individuals now fifty-three or older plan to retire before fifty-five, 25 percent of those under thirty-three do. When it comes to the desire to retire, the numbers are worse: 17 percent of those over fifty-three want to retire by the time they are fifty-five, while an astonishing 51 percent of those under thirty-three want to retire that early. The reason fewer older people plan to retire early may be due in part to their realization that they do not have the means to do so. Younger workers, who do not have to face that reality, are freer to

Table 1.1

Retirement Plans and Hopes of Current Workers

Age group in 1997	Plan to retire at 55 or earlier (%)	Want to retire at 55 or earlier (%)
All workers	15	33
53+	7	17
45–52	10	28
34–44	17	37
33 or younger	25	51

Source: Drawn from Paul Yakoboski and Jennifer Dickemper, "Increased Saving but Little Planning: Results of the 1997 Retirement Confidence Survey," *EBRI Issue Brief,* November 1997, p. 4, Chart 1.

assume that earlier retirement will somehow be affordable when they are ready for it.

New Definitions Offer New Hope

The good news is that surveys indicate that from half to almost three-quarters of boomers expect to work part-time in retirement. The numbers vary somewhat by income group, but in survey after survey, the majority of boomers who have made this decision do not indicate that they have done so because they believe that they will need the income.[3] Of course, these plans do not take into account the availability of such jobs, but if future retirees are adamant about abandoning full-time work, companies may be forced to respond to this preference. Mona Draper, chair of IEEE-USA's Engineering Employment Benefits Committee, believes that the "aging workforce is [already] making companies rethink how a business is run."[4] Few companies, however, have taken any serious action to build a model of work flexible enough to accommodate the desire of employees to work on very different schedules than those that still dominate in the current corporate workplace.

Looking Ahead

When those in charge of corporate America confront the problem of the coming tight labor markets and the need to entice more people into the workforce, they will need to do one more thing when it comes to the numbers: Break the baby boom into groups for further study. They will have to examine the experiences that shaped the attitudes of the members of the cohort at critical times in their life cycles, especially when it comes to the workplace. Just as siblings are affected by birth order, their family's income levels, their place of residence in their formative years, and the schools they attended (which is a result of both income and place of residence), so are members of any cohort that spans more than a few years.

Chapter 2

Breakdown: The Story Behind the Numbers

Listening to American workers of very different ages discuss their feelings about work and life reveals the problem facing corporate America in the first decades of the new millennium. These workers do not speak with one voice. Indeed, it is important to note the differences in the attitudes and decisions about work of each of these speakers—and to look at their ages. Those differences are a guide to some significant facts about the demographics we have been exploring.

The voice at the other end of the phone was cheery for the first time in weeks. "I just got the information I needed about the pension plan. If I retire at sixty, my pension will be enough to manage on until I can collect Social Security. It'll be tight and I'll have to use some savings, but I can do it."

Asked about finding a different job instead of retiring, she says, "I'm over the hill, no one will talk to me at my age. Besides, it won't be any better someplace else. I'm just so fed up, so tired of it all, I want out. I'm tired of waking up in the middle of the night worrying about getting this or that report ready. I'm tired of constantly trying to find new people to hire because everyone moves around so much. I guess I'm just tired of all the stress."

THE SPEAKER? The fifty-eight-year-old director of communications at a small college in New York City. She held two similar positions earlier in her career and was recruited for this job eight years ago because of her reputation.

In 1990, a good friend called to tell me she'd just been warned that the large Madison Avenue agency she worked for was downsizing again. She'd survived two previous downsizings, and each time had been depressed for months afterward. I asked what she was going to do and if I could help in any way. "Well, you probably can. I'm starting my own agency. I will not work for another large organization. My boys are at the age where I want to be part of their lives, coach their teams, just spend time with them. Will you take on an occasional assignment if I need help? My goal is to build a small company, using lots of freelance help so I don't have to worry about payrolls, overhead, those kinds of things. I want to be able to turn down assignments, especially those involving a lot of travel. You know me—I want to work hard but not the way I've been working."

THE SPEAKER? Then thirty-five, she is now the very successful forty-five-year-old president of the small agency she founded near her home in Connecticut. The agency has made a substantial profit every year for the past nine years but has not expanded as much as it could have. Currently, the permanent staff includes five full-time employees, including the president, and five part-timers. She has turned down two recent offers of senior marketing positions from Fortune 500 companies; the offers would pay her far more than she earns now.

During breaks in a series of communications seminars I was giving, I asked various members of the group why they had chosen to take the course. One participant said he'd tell me later, in private. When we spoke he said he didn't want to say anything publicly yet because "I'm going to give notice in a month. I'm planning to go back to college for a couple of years to pick up a master's. I'm tired of the rat race ... the twenty-hour days—and besides, my wife got a big promotion. We can make it on her salary, and I'll sell some stocks to pay for school. I desperately want to do something new, challenging and—more than anything—something that will make a difference. At any rate, I thought a course in communications would be useful for school."

THE SPEAKER? A twenty-eight-year-old former Silicon Valley computer programmer who made a great deal of money through stock options and who had recently received a promotion and raise.

Three voices, three demographic groups, three choices about work, one message. This raises an important issue about the way demographers define generations that needs exploration.

The Generational Divide

Demographic projections about the boomers are used in all kinds of forecasting, from the number of Social Security recipients to the population density of different areas of the country. Trend lines are developed based on the actions of earlier groups when they reached similar ages, but this does not always provide a sound guide to the future. The problem with trends is that people tend to break with the past in response to outside forces such as wars, economic depressions, or social movements—and how long that kind of behavior lasts and how dramatic the next swing will be are not predictable.

Another problem for those trying to forecast developments is that demographers divide populations into groups based on common statistical factors. Those born in the high birthrate years after World War II (starting in 1946) until the year that marked an abrupt drop in births (1964) are treated in demographic terminology as a single cohort—the baby boomers. The nineteen-year time span marking the baby boom also comes close to the parameters of a generation, that is, from the birth of the parents to the birth of their offspring—usually about twenty-five years. Thus, we hear about the swing generation (1900–26) or the silent generation (1927–45).[1]

There was a defining event for each of these groups—World War I for the swing generation, the Great Depression for the silent generation. When it comes to the boomers, however, instead of a single defining event, there was a cascade. For example, the first boomers were participants in or at least witnesses to the civil rights movement and the Vietnam War; the youngest boomers consider those events history. In fact, the first of the boomers have more in common with the war babies, who were very active in the protests of the 1960s, than they do with those born later in the boomer cohort, just as the last of the boomers have more in common with the members of the group known as Generation X, the smaller generation that came after the boomers.

In March 1996, USA Today's Andrea Stone described the youngest of the baby boomers, those twenty million boomers born in the early 1960s, as a "lost generation, stuck between Woodstock and Lollapalooza. Howdy Doody was canceled before most were born. They didn't wear Davy Crockett coonskin hats. They don't remember JFK's assassination. The Vietnam War ended before they reached the draft age. AIDS abolished free love." Some of this group "even have parents who are boomers," but they don't feel any connection to the boomers.[2]

Defining Moments

Although the media seem wedded to the notion of the baby boomers as a single entity, some demographers now treat the boomers as a divided population. They define the first boomer cohort as those born from 1946 to 1954, who came of age from 1963 to 1972. The defining moments for that cohort were, as noted above, the civil rights movement, economic good times, and the Vietnam War. The second half of the cohort, born from 1955 to 1965 and coming of age from 1973 to 1983, faced the declines in the economy brought about by the oil shocks of the 1970s and an end to the mindset, prompted by prosperity, of helping those who needed help. The world in which the second half of the boomer generation was raised was, in part, created by the first half. The formative years of the second cohort of boomers followed a period marked by intense rebellion. That rebellion brought about both a more open, freethinking mindset among many and also the "silent majority" that supported Richard Nixon, Ronald Reagan, and the Christian Right.

In addition, this second group of boomers is not as well-off financially as the first. When they entered the workforce, jobs were scarce as a result of the economic downturn that had begun in the early 1980s. Consequently, many in this group have spent a number of years doing work that is "second best." For example, many people with graduate degrees are teaching adjuncts at two or three colleges, spending as many hours at work as tenured professors for one-third the salary and no possibility of advancement. In fact, in the 1980s, 20 percent of those who graduated from college found themselves unemployed or working in jobs that did not require their hard-won, expensive degrees.[3]

Another disadvantage experienced by this group was that by the time they were ready to set up their own households, buying a home was beyond their reach. Therefore, they are entering their late thirties with far less equity than the first group of boomers. In *The Master Trend,* Cheryl Russell, a demographer who has long studied the boomers, points out that "people who bought homes in the mid-1970s, for example, took on a mortgage payment of just over $300 a month, or 24 percent of their monthly income. Those buying homes in the late 1980s were strapped with a mortgage payment of over $1000 a month, amounting to one-third of their monthly income." She goes on to explain that even with the fall in interest rates in the 1990s, those who bought before 1980 still got a better bargain.[4]

It is not surprising then that the later boomers and many in the first wave of Generation X turned from work to other aspects of their lives to find satisfaction. As a group, they tend to focus on personal growth and look internally for values. Many were children of divorce, raised in single-parent families or in families that were far from traditional, with step- and half brothers and sisters, and so today they put family life ahead of many other values.

When it comes to work, this group is determined to spend time honing new skills and pursuing personal interests that could lead to alternative careers. And because these young boomers are technoliterate, often technophiles, the possibilities of entrepreneurship are an integral part of their mindset. They see an example of success not just in the new generation of Internet businesses but in the example of the founders and heads of some of the most powerful technology companies in the world—all boomers born in the mid-1950s: Bill Gates of Microsoft, Scott McNealy of Sun Microsystems, Steve Wozniak of Apple. Of the seven million adults launching their own businesses in the mid-1990s, almost 80 percent were under thirty-four.[5]

Despite this drive to entrepreneurship, most of those in this younger group do not believe that they will ever have enough money to retire completely. At the same time, there seems to be a great deal of cynicism about the future that keeps them from working the endless hours needed to remedy that. They believe the solution is to retire from the work they do as early as possible, then start doing something else after that first formal retirement. In 1997, the Employee Benefit Research Institute looked at the retirement plans of workers from war babies (immediate pre-boomers) to Generation X (immediate postboomers). They found that although the youngest boomers and Generation Xers expect and want to retire early in record numbers, almost three-quarters also expect to work at least part-time when retired.[6] Since they know that nothing in the world of work stays the same for long, moving on to something else strikes them as only natural.

Perhaps most important to those who will need employees when the oldest boomers begin to retire, these younger boomers and Generation Xers are much less likely to join large organizations. For most, moving in and out of the workforce, often going from job to job to learn new skills or setting up small businesses of their own, seems a more sensible course of action. They do not believe that the stresses and demands of work in large corporations offer much in return.

Looking Deeper

In general, with regard to boomers and their feelings about the workplace, demographic groupings are particularly misleading. To understand what it will take to keep boomers working for an organization, it is important to break down this huge cohort into fairly small groups, keeping in mind their ages during the corporate upheavals of the late 1980s and early 1990s. (The shaded area in Table 2.1 is the reference point for the descriptions of what each of the smaller groups within the boomer and surrounding cohorts encountered at work.)

THE WAR BABIES AND FIRST BOOMERS

The war babies and first boomers, the children of those employed in the paternalistic organizations of the mid-1940s through 1960s, had expectations of work that included a solid career ladder—or

Table 2.1

Where Were You When the World of Work Changed?[a]

Birth cohort	Ages at given years					
	1960	1970	1980	1990	2000	2010
War babies (1940–45)	15–20	25–30	35–40	45–50	55–60	65–70
First boomers (1945–50)	10–15	20–25	30–35	40–45	50–55	60–65
Early boomers (1950–55)	5–10	15–20	25–30	35–40	45–50	55–60
Second wave (1955–60)	0–5	10–15	20–25	30–35	40–45	50–55
Last boomers (1960–65)	n.a.	5–10	15–20	25–30	35–40	45–50
Generation X (1965–70)	n.a.	0–5	10–15	20–25	30–35	40–45

[a]The shaded area represents the point at which the new world of work started taking shape as companies downsized and remade themselves in response to competition.

Source: Author's calculations.

at least rewards for seniority—a need for occasional (but not dramatic) upgrading of skills, good pensions, and steady benefits. In return, they were loyal to their employers and cared about their organizations. These were the children whose parents had either lived through or been taught the lessons of the Great Depression—that security was next to godliness.

The members of these groups, who were thirty-five to forty-five during the corporate upheavals of the late 1980s and early 1990s, had joined the workforce believing that the world of work experienced by their parents was the norm. And when they began their careers it seemed as though it would remain so. Hence their shock and disbelief when just as they were finally moving up the career ladder, or at least had enough seniority with an organization to feel secure, their world suddenly seemed to turn upside down.

The career ladder was smashed along with hierarchies; downsizings involved whole divisions and even whole plants, making seniority moot and work at anything close to the same level hard to find for those who had lost their jobs.

The Early Boomers

The early boomers had different experiences. Ranging in age from thirty to thirty-five during the upheavals, they had already experienced some hard knocks in the world of work; many began their first jobs in the late 1970s, when jobs were becoming less plentiful because of increased global competitiveness and worldwide economic difficulties. They were at the point in their careers during the upheavals when they were still changing jobs in the search for advancement, an employment pattern typical of younger workers finding their way. They had to accept that the constant change taking place was not going to end.

The Second Wave

The second wave had still different experiences. When they entered the world of work, jobs were not plentiful because a huge workforce of boomers was already in place and a global economic downturn had begun. But many of those who found jobs recognized that the new technologies being rapidly adopted were the wave of the future, and they seized every opportunity to learn how to use these new systems. Yet when the upheavals began, they frequently found themselves quickly out of work—"last hired, first fired."

THE LAST BOOMERS AND GENERATION X

Most members of these groups had not yet entered the workforce when the upheavals began, but they were affected by them anyway. Their parents suddenly weren't certain about whether or for how long they could help finance a college education. Having witnessed what had happened to the world of work, they made very different choices about what kind of organizations they wanted to work for. Many of this group had strong technological skills and preferred taking the risks involved in starting their own businesses or at least being part of new start-ups. Those who joined corporations understood the need to learn new skills constantly and to switch jobs frequently to get training. Today, they neither expect nor seek corporate loyalty. The most significant workforce commitment factor for these younger workers, according to a survey of some 1,800 workers by Aon Consulting of Chicago, is "management's recognition of the importance of personal and family life." For workers over forty, benefits are first, ranked as "equal to, or greater than, pay."[7]

We Want to Work, but for Ourselves

Maybe it's the image of the garage—well, if not the garage, a dorm room or den—the places where so many Silicon Valley giants such as Hewlett-Packard, Dell, and Microsoft were born, that is shaping the idea of what work means today. The entrepreneurial spirit is alive and well among many segments of boomers, from older boomers who decide to become consultants to younger ones searching for investors to finance a new idea for a technologically based service.

This entrepreneurial mindset is embraced most strongly by the youngest boomers and Generation Xers. About 10 percent of Americans between the ages of twenty-five and thirty-four are now involved in businesses of their own (three times the number of any other age group), and surveys by such groups as the Young Entrepreneurs Network indicate that those numbers are likely to grow dramatically. College students are preparing themselves for a future in which they own their own businesses: In 1970, sixteen universities offered degree programs for entrepreneurs; In 1996, four hundred did.[8]

These changes in the world of work have brought about a shift in the model of employment that has raised questions, especially from managers wedded to the older model, about its durability and workability. Looking at the model in a historical context should answer those questions. For although a sharp break with the model that dominated in the industrial age, it is a workable model that is similar in many ways to the model of work that dominated in the agricultural age (see Table 2.2). Examining the various elements of the model makes it clear why younger boomers, who never experienced the industrial model at its best, are likely to embrace this new model and what that means for corporations:

Time. In the agricultural age, work was controlled to a large extent by nature. It had to be done in daylight, and crafts were easiest to sell when farmers had in hand the profits from selling their crops. Moreover, within the confines of nature, work could be done when one pleased because it was done independently of others. In the industrial age, factories and the assembly line made that impossible. With the development of new communications

Table 2.2

Changes in the World of Work

	Agricultural	Industrial	Information
Time	Natural and self-directed	Inflexible	Self-directed
Energy	Physical	Physical and mental	Mental
Management	Independent	Paternalist	Personally chosen
Creativity and innovation	Little scope	Limited	Demanded
Job stability	High	High	Low
Rewards	Uncertain	Certain	Uncertain
Independence	High	Low	High

Source: Beverly Goldberg, *Overcoming High-Tech Anxiety: Thriving in a Wired World* (San Francisco: Jossey-Bass, 1999), p. 61.

and information technology, a large degree of freedom has been restored. A great deal of work can now be done when it is convenient for the worker, within given parameters, especially if done at home.

Energy. As corporations move more of their manufacturing facilities abroad, the hard physical labor that marked the agricultural and industrial ages is disappearing. Much of the work of the companies of the information age requires the expenditure of brain power rather than muscle power.

Management. In the agricultural age, most people were free to manage their own plot of land in their own way, so long as they produced at least enough to feed their families and pay taxes. Craft workers were free to produce as much or as little as they needed, so long as they earned enough to support themselves. Once technology made farming far less labor-intensive and brought about the growth of industry, this model was replaced by employment by others. After all, manufacturing, because it took huge investments in plant and materials, was not something individuals could decide to do on their own. Now technological advances and corporate decisions to move plants abroad have brought about a reduction in the size of the U.S.-based manufacturing sector and an increase in the service sector, including businesses that can provide services and products without large initial investments. People can once again choose to work for themselves.

Creativity and Innovation. Unless one was involved in an artistic endeavor or was a craftsman, there was little scope for creativity in the agricultural age. In the industrial age, the assembly-line worker was just a pair of hands performing a specific function, but there was room for creativity in fields such as marketing and advertising. In addition, as products became commodities, creative design became more important. In the information age, companies are open to new and creative approaches on every front, especially those centering on technological innovation.

Job Stability. In the agricultural age, the same skills were usually in demand over a lifetime. In the industrial age, basic skills might have to be upgraded, but most jobs remained the same over time. Today, not only do jobs disappear with little warning, but the skills needed for some of them change so dramatically and so often that the jobs come to seem totally different. Moreover, new jobs are constantly created through technology and in the field of technology.

Rewards. The agricultural age offered no guarantees of financial rewards. A long drought or a flood could impoverish a farmer—and those who provided the goods that farmers usually bought. In the industrial age, work was rewarded by a weekly paycheck. As nations became more industrialized, social safety nets were put in place and unions were created to protect workers. Later in the industrial age, companies routinely provided benefits and severance pay when laying off workers. In the information age, there is a return to the older model, with workers moving from job to job with few assurances of long-term employment or benefits.

Independence. The information age is bringing a return to a more independent way of life. Ownership of the tools of one's trade (usually a computer) and transferable skill sets are once again enabling workers to market themselves in very different ways. Contingent work and entrepreneurship provide rewards for those who do not want to depend on others for their security. The corporate shift to outsourcing has made this alternative easier for those attracted to the entrepreneurial life.

The Ticking Time Bomb

This new model of work will pose an enormous problem for corporations in the early years of the twenty-first century, when large organizations will have to find workers to maintain productivity and growth as the workforce grows older. Susan MacManus notes in *Young v. Old: Generational Combat in the 21st Century* that Americans now fifty and older "control 70 percent of the country's wealth, yet comprise only 25 percent of the population."[9] They are fairly free to choose to retire. Companies will have to find ways to make work as pleasant as possible to attract these people back into the very organizations that forced out so many of their peers.

The first group of boomers presents a somewhat different picture from the war babies; they have done fairly well, can afford to retire, but seem interested in staying involved. These boomers are part of the "youth culture" and want to remain young—at least to feel young. They are likely to choose to be free agents, working, but only when they want to, once they near or pass retirement age.

There are large numbers of women in this group, many of whom have found work extremely attractive and would like to stay employed even after their spouses opt for retirement. Surveys by Catalyst, a New York–based national nonprofit research and advisory organization aimed at helping women in business and the professions, reveal that women want flexibility above all else, time to vacation with retired spouses, visit grandchildren, participate in community affairs, and do volunteer work. Others have found that divorce, downsizing, and lack of investment know-how have left them with far less income than they will need to retire comfortably, and so they are likely to remain at work. The number involved is not large enough to ease the coming shortfalls in the labor market.[10]

Adding to the shortages that will be created if the war babies' and first boomers' desire for flexibility isn't met and they retire as soon as they can is the different mindset about work held by the youngest boomers. Although these younger boomers are likely to remain at work through the first years of the retirement of the older boomers, they tend not to feel the need to put in endless extra hours for a company for which they have no particular loyalty. Rather, they think of every job they hold as temporary—even when those jobs are classified as full-time permanent jobs. They feel free to move on to more interesting work whenever an opportunity to do so presents itself. Moreover, these younger boomers, like Generation Xers, do not particularly want to work for large organizations. Many of them prefer smaller organizations and leave the workplace from time to time to explore new fields and pursue additional training and education.

There is a strange irony in the fact that the only way to keep these individuals at work will be to provide them with opportunities to arrange flexible work lives. In other words, corporate

America must offer its workers exactly what it created in terms of its own structures—flexibility.

Business faces the danger that it may wait too long to wake up to this enormous—and inevitable—problem. Companies are still focusing on the short-term, aware of but not paying a lot of attention to the possible ramifications of the coming retirement of all those baby boomers. George Bailey, the global director of the Human Capital Group at Watson Wyatt Worldwide, says that a study of U.S. employers in 1997 revealed that only 11 percent of CEOs recognize that a "major management challenge in coming years will be the shortage of younger workers. . . . Younger generations of workers will sell their skills to the highest bidder."[11]

Dealing with the Fallout

Given the numbers, whether or not the current economic boom continues, workers will have to be convinced to remain in the workplace a while longer. For this, three things must happen:

- Those workers facing the third phase of their lives, a phase that will be far longer than that enjoyed by any generation before them, must be encouraged to think about what they want their lives to consist of in the years ahead—paid work, retirement, volunteering, or a mixture, and what that mixture will include.
- Corporations must come to a greater understanding of the labor requirements of the new flexible organizations they have created, and how work can be structured in those flexible organizations so workers will be willing to stay on in some capacity, ensuring that corporations will have the labor forces they need when they need them.
- Policymakers must be prepared to facilitate the changes needed by putting in place education, retirement, and health policies compatible with the new world of work.

Moreover, if our economy is to flourish, those entering retirement without ample means will need at some point to earn enough to be consumers. Part of the battle will be to convince those retiring without adequate funds that, since at some future date they will have to find more money, staying at work a while longer makes more sense than relying on returning to work if they live longer than they can afford to. As the years pass, they are less likely to have the stamina to work and their skills will be inadequate. The other side of the coin is convincing corporate America that it must begin now to face the issues involved in the graying of the workforce.

Part II

The Causes

Chapter 3

Downsized, Displaced, and Disillusioned

"I'm so nervous about this merger. If it goes through, so many people will be laid off. Even if I'm not let go, living through another round of firings is so depressing. This time, if I get a good buyout deal—I think I'll take it."

"I really don't think I can face learning another new set of programs—it's the second time this year I'll be at a 'boot camp.' So I called to find out how much my pension would pay if I retire when I hit fifty-nine-and-a-half. Oh, I'll still have to go through the training, but if I know getting out in a few years is realistic, it'll be easier."

"All I want is out . . . but I don't have enough saved up to take some time off to figure out what to do next. . . . I'll have to stick around, but I just don't care a lot—about the company, or my job."

Escaping from the workforce is clearly on many workers' minds. If corporate America is going to find ways to combat this planned exodus from work as the baby boomers near retirement age, it must begin to understand its causes. The most obvious are the cascade of changes that began to remake the world of work in the mid- to late 1980s as American businesses struggled to rebuild in response to the losses they had suffered from the international economic downturn that began in the 1970s. Moreover, the remodeling and restructuring of the workplace that began in response to that downturn has never slowed; it continues today.

The changes that shook the world of work in the last quarter of the twentieth century can best be described as "churning"—a seemingly constant demand for workers with new skills to do new kinds of work as old processes, technologies, and ways of doing business were constantly replaced by new ones. While unemployment today is lower than it has been in decades, in large part owing to the creation of new jobs, people constantly find that their old jobs are disappearing. The new work they find comes with lower salaries and fewer benefits, and the need to learn additional skills never ends.

In addition, today's leaner workplaces—the result of an organizational focus on little but the bottom line—are stressful to work in, demanding long hours and a defensive mentality. *Business Week* reports that in 1990, almost 20 percent of employees indicated that they were frequently concerned about being laid off; by 1994, the number had more than doubled, and it remains over 40 percent today.[1]

Is all of this unhappiness and anxiety justified?

- Labor Department statistics put the number of jobs eliminated between 1979 and 1993 at thirty-six million.[2]
- Some 2.2 million workers were laid off in 1993 and 1994; only two-thirds had found full-time jobs by 1996, and more than half of those workers earned less than they did in their former jobs, with nearly one-third earning at least 20 percent less.[3]
- On average, older workers who lose their jobs have a hard time finding new positions; in a February 1998 survey, the Bureau of

Labor Statistics reported that 82 percent of displaced workers aged twenty-five to fifty-four were reemployed, while only 60 percent of those aged fifty-five to sixty-four were, and just 35 percent of those over sixty-four had found new employment.[4]

The uncertainty, anxiety, and frustration about work that drives people to look for ways to escape are direct responses to these numbers. The way workers have been treated by businesses trying to rebuild has resulted in the disappearance of the old social contract between employers and employees, which involved rights, obligations, and loyalty. But the biggest problem may prove to be the failure to develop a new contract to take its place.

In the face of the uncertainty that has replaced decades of comfortable work arrangements, employees who think that somehow they can muddle through the rest of their lives with some degree of financial security are deciding that they have had enough. Many downsized older employees have given up searching for work. Many workers who have had to settle for new jobs that offer less status, power, and income are waiting anxiously for the day they can opt out. Others are resigned to holding on to the job they have as long as they can, but they invest as little of themselves in it as possible.

These disaffected workers who continue to work do not care about the future of the companies for which they work. They have little interest in searching for creative solutions to problems, learning new ways of working, or going the extra mile to make sure a deadline is met. In fact, they often resist learning new technologies, making it difficult for companies to evaluate the benefits of these technologies with any degree of accuracy.

The danger is that, if something is not done to change these attitudes, older workers marking time and performing at minimal levels are going to adversely impact corporate performance. Such attitudes, after all, tend to affect everyone in the organization, often causing more enthusiastic new workers to lose heart quickly.

Finding ways to change the attitudes of workers doing little more than waiting to retire will become increasingly important as we enter the first decades of the new millennium, because older workers will represent an ever-larger percentage of the workforce as the entire population ages.

Another aspect of the problem is the shift from the industrial age to the information age, from manufacturing to service industries. Companies have moved their manufacturing abroad, shrinking the number of blue-collar jobs that once were the road to a solid middle-class life. Most of the service-sector jobs that have replaced work in manufacturing do not provide the same income. Although these changes were a result of challenges to American business by competition from other nations, these decisions, which frequently severed the relationship between corporation and employee, were often poorly implemented. This left loyal employees scrambling for new work and brought little in the way of solid financial rewards to those who remained.

This loss of real income has been widely covered by the media. One leading economist reporting on the development, Edward Wolff of New York University, noted that there was a "drop in mean and medium real income between 1989 and 1992. Indeed, between 1983 and 1992, the bottom 80 percent of households, as ranked in terms of income, suffered an absolute decline in their average real income. Only the top 20 percent saw their incomes rise over the period. Between 1983 and 1992, over 100 percent of the growth of income went into the hands of the top 20 percent of income recipients and almost two-thirds to the top 1 percent."[5]

The forces that mandated change, the types of changes made, and the effects of these changes (some a matter of perception, others of bitter reality) have brought about a new world of work that requires a very different mindset from the old one. The problem is that the resentment and anger in the wake of these changes makes developing such a mindset extremely difficult.

The Origins of the New World of Work

America, the land of opportunity, blessed with natural resources and the entrepreneurial spirit, suffered a devastating blow to its position as the world's economic leader in the 1970s in the face of international struggles and increased business competition from other nations, such as Japan. During those years, America's belief in its own superiority was sorely tested, and it took more than a decade for American business to regroup and begin to put in place the new technologies, processes, and management practices that eventually restored it to world leadership. Those years of floundering and experimentation with one new solution after another were extremely painful for employees and created much of the current anxiety and distrust that marks today's workforce.

A Place of Prosperity

This nation's history is marked by the belief that everyone has unlimited opportunities to achieve success and that the members of every generation can build a better life than their parents did. Over the decades, a middle class emerged that was at the heart of America's strength, and that class grew dramatically in the years following World War II. The opportunity to better oneself was largely a result of the benefits offered to returning veterans, the global demand for U.S. goods after the war, and the innovations made possible by research done as part of the war effort that brought about technological advances.

For example, in the post–World War II period, veterans were provided with a number of benefits that made achieving the American dream far easier than ever before. The GI Bill of Rights provided returning veterans with housing loans, which turned a nation of renters into homeowners, and boosted the national economy as housing construction boomed along with the industries that provided the furnishings and appliances for those homes. It also provided education and training benefits that led some 6.6 million veterans to attend some kind of vocational school or degree-granting institution. (More than 1.2 million veterans attended colleges and universities.[6]) The result was the world's best-educated workforce.

Those veterans became the heart of the workforce that made possible the growth and expansion of the U.S. industrial base in the postwar period. They helped American industry meet the pent-up demand for goods that the factories of Europe and Asia, devastated by the war, were unable to supply. U.S. businesses quickly retooled the plants that, during the war, had been turned into suppliers of military goods, and the United States became the world's principal supplier of manufactured goods.

In fact, by 1953 U.S. manufacturing accounted for 53 percent of world manufacturing output. In that environment, it was possible for companies to expand and grow, increasing the size of their workforces. In a world in which the quantity of goods one could produce was the critical factor in achieving success, companies felt no need to rein in the benefits that had lured scarce workers during the war, when the War Labor Board froze salaries.[7] This, combined with the strong union presence in the manufacturing sector, meant that American workers prospered.

Michael Barone, long-time reporter for *U.S. News and World Report,* notes that the "one-fifth of American families with the highest incomes received 54% of total income in 1929, 52% in 1935–36, and 46% in 1944—fairly small statistical changes that signaled huge shifts in flows of billions of dollars. The share of total income received by the bottom three-fifths rose from 26% in 1929 to 27% in 1935–36 to 32% in 1944."[8] During these years, American workers developed a belief in the rewards of the system: Hard work and loyalty to one's employer brought good salaries and benefits, opportunities for promotions, and, eventually, a comfortable retirement.

We were also a generous nation at that time, providing in our prosperity for those who had less. We supported the regrowth of Europe through the Marshall Plan; we built schools for the enormous generation of baby boomers who were born during those good years after the war; we put in place social programs for the poor, including welfare, Head Start, and public housing. We even began to redress the wrongs done to minorities.

They're on Our Tail

Everything began to change in the 1970s. Our prosecution of the Vietnam War and the cost of supporting the massive social programs put in place in the 1960s drove the country into massive debt. Global competition began to damage our balance of trade. Those nations that produced the oil the United States consumed joined together to push up prices. Japan and Europe built new plants that were more efficient and more technologically advanced than our old, refurbished plants, and they adopted new management practices aimed at efficiency.

In Japan, management expert W. Edwards Deming, whose ideas about quality had been rejected in America, found an audience for his theories. The improved quality of Japanese automobiles and their more fuel-efficient design (especially important as oil prices rose) meant that, by the end of the 1970s, American automobile manufacturers had lost almost a third of their market to Japanese imports.

Over the next decade, American companies of all kinds faced intense competition from abroad. "Made in America" no longer meant the best or most advanced product; Japanese and then German automobiles were followed by Japanese televisions and other electronic goods, and then the Japanese began to corner the all-important computer chip market. Not only were such goods from abroad manufactured to higher standards, but they cost less as well.

At the same time, the technological innovations that resulted in large part from enormous U.S. government-funded research and development programs, both during the war and in the cold war era that followed, provided other nations with the ability to reverse-engineer products. According to *Business Week,* "a U.S. company can easily spend, say, $1 million developing a new product only to watch helplessly as lower-cost imitations flood the market before the product reached breakeven."[9] And in areas where cost was more of a consideration than quality, such as children's clothing, the availability of cheap labor helped foreign companies win a huge share of the American market. American business was reeling.

Let the Race Begin

The response to the shock of no longer being number one, especially in steel and automobile manufacturing (industries Americans believed they owned), was more than a decade of frenzied attempts to regain the lead. Corporations searched for quick fixes and seemed impervious to the fact that the global business environment was in the midst of a permanent alteration as a result of changes in technology, markets, and consumer demand.

In the search for solutions, the most startling fact that emerged from an examination of Japanese manufacturing methods was the difference in defect rates, which were about "a tenth of their American competitors'."[10] As a result, many American managers decided that improving quality was the solution to their problems. At the same time, America's corporate leadership realized that the new plants built abroad utilized advanced technology, and so many embarked on a drive to add new technologies to increase productivity. Companies made changes so quickly that many new methods and processes were implemented with little thought as to how they would affect the company overall or how such changes should be managed. Not surprisingly, many of the changes failed to bring about the expected improvements.

False Starts and Solid Beginnings

On the surface, it seemed to make sense to look to the Japanese model for ways to solve our problems, but there were two major flaws in this idea. First, according to Robert J. Crawford, a former policy analyst at the U.S. National Science Foundation's Tokyo office, the focus on management style tended to "neglect the larger context of trade and industrial policies," which protected Japanese industries from competition.[11] Second, there was a great deal of misinterpretation about what was actually happening in the Japanese corporate world. In the rush to regain lost ground, U.S. companies moved too quickly to emulate what they imagined were perfect solutions, ignoring cultural differences that affected outcomes and making many other mistakes. However, many of those mistakes were to prove beneficial in the long run because they moved companies in new directions that ultimately brought about a new organizational model—one that did, finally, make a difference.

PLAYING TOGETHER

The first big change made as a result of the examination of Japanese competitors was the adoption of the team concept. Although the Japanese programs never quite worked as well here, managers eventually realized that teams were, in the words of consultants Jon Katzenbach and Douglas Smith, "more flexible than larger organizational groupings because they can be more quickly assembled, deployed, refocused, and disbanded. . . . In any situation requiring the real-time combination of multiple skills, experiences, and judgments, a team invariably gets better results than a collection of individuals operating within confined job roles and responsibilities."[12] After many wrong turns, the team concept was finally adopted for the American workplace.

The use of teams brought many advantages. One that had important consequences was cross-training. By teaching every member of a team how to do each of the tasks required for a given stage in manufacturing or the production of services, companies achieved far greater flexibility. Workers learned new skills, but perhaps more important for their futures, these new skills made it easier for them to move into new jobs. This approach also made it possible for companies that were desperate to retrieve some of the money spent on new technologies to shrink their full-time workforces; each member of the team was capable of doing more than one part of the process when demand was slow, and temporary workers could be called in to augment the workforce when demand increased.

These downsizings were an unintended consequence. Actions taken for one purpose often produce quite unexpected results, which are beneficial to some, harmful to others. For example, the push to emulate the Japanese focus on quality through the adoption of quality circles made the switch to less hierarchical corporate structures easier, as workers who spent time on teams gained skills in negotiating and communicating that were once the exclusive province of managers. While this benefited companies by making it possible for them to reduce the number of their middle managers, it harmed those whose career path was in middle management.

Let the Machine Do It

At the same time all this was happening, changes were taking place as a result of technological advances. The developments in technology, particularly in computers, that had begun during World War II continued and finally began to enter the workplace in the early 1980s. When it came to manufacturing, American companies, all too aware of the so-called robotic factories that had been built in Japan, again rushed to emulate the Japanese model. Companies invested billions of dollars in high-tech equipment and automation. However, because the decisions about what to automate were not always carefully thought through, it took far longer than expected to achieve the desired improvements in productivity—and some of these companies simply did not have the time, given the competitive battleground that had developed.

The fastest gains from technology came from its use in streamlining back-office operations. Unfortunately, once the march to computerization had begun, companies again hopped on a bandwagon with little caution. Many organizations acquired computers in massive numbers at massive costs, only to have those computers then spend years sitting on the desks of untrained, resistant workers. Companies did not understand that technology had to be integrated into a comprehensive strategic plan, or that the corporate culture had to be changed to gain acceptance of this new way of working, and that people had to be carefully trained to use these new devices. Not until the late 1980s did the idea of aligning business and technology strategy and structure really take hold.[13]

With change management and training—and advances in computer technology that made these machines far more user-friendly—workers soon found themselves comfortable with the specific programs that related to their jobs. In fact, once these technologies were implemented properly, their value became clear. Technology brought about the automation of many time-consuming tasks once done by hand by a good part of the workforce. Because far fewer workers could now do these tasks, the costs of back-office operations such as payroll, accounts payable, and budgeting dropped from a little over 2 percent of revenues in 1988 to half that amount in 1998.[14] Technology also made possible record-keeping that facilitated the reorganization of the processes used within the organization, again eliminating the need for layers of management—and for workers.

There's Always Another Way

Business process reengineering, one of the critical phases of the revolution in corporate operations, also played a critical role in creating the new workplace. While U.S. businesses were in the midst of their desperate search for solutions, Michael Hammer's article "Reengineering Work: Don't Automate, Obliterate" appeared in the influential *Harvard Business Review*.[15] The idea that a company could increase profitability by analyzing each step of a process to reduce inefficiencies and eliminate redundancies became the holy grail of management.

Companies accepted the proposition that they could increase profitability by eliminating unnecessary steps in the production process and the workers who performed them. When business process reengineering was implemented without changes in overall strategy and without proper change management efforts, however, it resulted in failure about 70 percent of the time. And the downsizings created by reengineering did not bring many long-term returns: The American Management Association announced in 1993 that only 44 percent of companies reported an increase in operating profits following downsizing; 47 percent reported a decrease or no change.[16]

Eventually, as more companies found ways to reengineer successfully, these efforts—especially when combined with the adoption of new technology—did improve operations. Reengineering also had unexpected consequences. The announcement that reengineering was under way and that payroll reductions were likely led to an immediate increase in the value of a company's stock, a fact that senior management took very much to heart the next time they faced the possibility of poor quarterly returns.

Downsized, Displaced, and Disillusioned

EMPOWERED AND ELIMINATED

Perhaps the most unnerving development during this period when companies were trying, often simultaneously, every new "silver bullet" that was put forth was the flattening of the hierarchical structures that were at the heart of the growth of middle management. There are many explanations for why the managerial ranks in corporations were so large and multilayered. One was that many layers of oversight were needed because ordinary workers could not be trusted with the responsibility for communicating with one another and up and down the chain of command in the organization. Another was that people who worked their way up the supervisory chain would learn what it took to make the organization run; in other words, it was a way to train people and determine who should move up the corporate ladder. Yet another explanation was that because managers were rewarded for the number of people who reported to them, the more layers they put in place, the more managerial they looked.

This command-and-control system, which worked very well in large manufacturing organizations, did not work well in service-sector companies where rapid response to clients was the critical success factor. The multilayers of management that had to sign off on decisions slowed things down. The added costs of so many managers hurt companies facing new competitors with leaner organizational structures. Moreover, managers were so involved in the minutiae of overseeing specific tasks that they lost sight of the larger strategic goals of the organization.

Charles Heckscher points out in *White-Collar Blues* that the history of the large command-and-control organizations of the 1950s made it unlikely that these managers would change the way they did things. In these organizations, managers "were treated as permanent members of permanent enterprises. They were paid well and could confidently expect careers of steadily increasing responsibility and rewards."[17] These managers were loyal to their organizations and expected their loyalty to be rewarded—as long as they continued to do what was expected of them. Now, confronted by a need to change, they simply did not understand what was expected and felt betrayed by the changes taking place around them.

Companies quickly found solutions to the problem of huge bureaucracies that tended to stymie growth and change. They empowered good workers at every level with more decision-making responsibility and accountability, eliminating the need for so much oversight and decision making by those without specific, task-oriented skills. At the same time, U.S. businesses began to consolidate. Mergers and acquisitions, strategic alliances, and cooperative ventures were happening in every industry as companies tried to take greater advantage of economies of scale to keep up with global competition. As companies merged, managers with responsibilities similar to those of their counterparts in the opposite firm were eliminated, which further reduced the ranks of middle management.

Those caught up in these changes, especially in the merger frenzy, felt betrayed by a world they did not understand. What was worse was the failure of organizations to deal with those downsized in such a way that the breaking of the old social contract was at least acknowledged (see Box 3.1).

Doing Only What You Do Best

Another major change came when Gary Hamel and C. K. Prahalad introduced the concept of core competencies in their best-selling book, *Competing for the Future*. Core competencies proved the final blow to the huge organizational entities that maintained large enough internal managerial staffs and workers to perform every function entailed in bringing products or services to the customer. Businesses rapidly adopted the idea that an organization should focus on those things it did the best—its core competencies—

Box 3.1
Merger Mania:
Chase Manhattan Corporation
and Chemical Banking Corporation

In 1996, the mergers that had brought turmoil and change to the banking industry were continuing at a rapid pace. Banking was being remade by technology. The old rules and old ways of working were disappearing, a change most visible in the replacement of bank tellers with ATMs on every corner. When Chemical bought Chase for $10 billion in March 1996, the announcement was accompanied by the news that one hundred of the almost five hundred branches of the two banks would close and that twelve thousand jobs would be cut.

Morale plummeted. Not only were jobs on the line, but since this was not the first merger for either company and the previous year had been marked by a dozen major bank mergers, new banking jobs would not be easy to find. Hoping to alleviate some of the anger and paralysis that accompanied the news, Chase (Chemical bought the company but decided to use the Chase name) put a lot of effort into programs aimed at making people feel better. It instituted a Vision Quest program aimed at determining then proclaiming the values and goals of the organization—and inscribing them on everything, including the Styrofoam coffee cups at the company coffee stations. It also set up Career Vision, a program that was supposed to help employees acquire new skills they could take with them if they were among the downsized. These programs failed. In an article in the *New York Times,* N. R. Kleinfield quoted a Chase vice president as saying: "To a lot of us, Career Vision is like the Energizer Rabbit clickety-clacking through Bosnia."

Once management chose which employees to keep and which to let go, Chase managers were given scripts to guide them through the process of informing people that they were being downsized. The human resources department then handled the final work. One memorable story involves a human resource manager collecting a newly laid off employee's corporate ID and explaining to her that she'd be losing her free Chase checking account. Then, the manager handed her an application for a regular account.

The survivors were also unhappy. Discussing the post-merger workload, one employee said: "In the old days, it was nine to five with room for lunch. Now it's nine to ten with time for lunch every now and then. A lot of people in this bank are saying to themselves, 'If I survive this new merger, do I even want the job?' "

Perhaps most telling about the prevailing attitudes were comments by Thomas Labrecque, the chief executive of Chase during this period. Labrecque explained that those who found the new world of work too uncomfortable would simply have to leave. He pointed out that he'd heard from people who had left and were working for charities at half the salary, and that they were "happy." He admitted that what was happening was difficult, but explained it was for the greater good.

Chase also hired a nationwide outplacement firm. With jobs in banking so hard to find, downsized employees spent a great deal of time in the offices provided by the outplacement firm, offices marked by an air of gloom. Moreover, the outplacement firm structured these temporary offices to be uninviting to discourage people from getting comfortable. Perhaps one of the most revealing comments, in light of the tight labor markets ahead, was from a twenty-five-year-old retained employee: "Most people my age come to work for a big company with the intention of getting the training and acquiring the skills they need to move on . . . to either own their own company or work for a smaller company. People really don't have the loyalty they used to to a big company." Does anyone hearing these stories wonder why?

Source: N.R. Kleinfield, "A New and Unnerving Workplace," in New York Times, *The Downsizing of America* (New York: Times Books, 1996), pp. 37–76.

leaving those things in which it did not excel to other organizations. Companies turned to outsourcers, alliance partners, and various arrangements with contingent and temporary workers. The individuals and smaller organizations doing the outsourcing were considered interchangeable components. Flexibility had become the new corporate mantra.

All these changes were enabled by advances in technology, especially electronic business networking, which created fast links between corporations and the outsourcers and suppliers with whom they worked. This movement to a more virtual organizational form made it easier and easier not to hire permanent workers. Instead, companies construct a variety of work arrangements with people who are not considered a part of the organization. Unfortunately, many contingent or temporary workers are former insiders, now earning less than they earned before for the same work.

Checking the Twists and Turns to Be Navigated

Eventually, the plethora of quick fixes began to yield results. As each new quick fix was tried, some piece proved valuable. Organizations discovered their own roads to success. Companies learned that there were no silver bullets but rather directions to move in, ways to adapt, technologies that made a difference. Everyone lived through pronouncements about the coming of the virtual corporation, the takeover of the world by huge conglomerates, the total destruction of America's economy as manufacturing moved abroad. To some extent, these all had a bearing on the ultimate shape of American business as the 1990s drew to a close.

The Services Supreme

Another major change took place during the last decades of the twentieth century that added to the problems of the American worker. As companies began to move labor-intensive manufacturing operations abroad, more and more American workers found themselves doing a very different kind of work. In 1950, about 15 percent of the workforce was engaged in farming, 30 percent in manufacturing, and 50 percent in the service sector. Today, those numbers have changed dramatically: A scant 5 percent of the workforce is engaged in farming, 15 percent in manufacturing, and almost 80 percent in the service sector. The goods sector (which includes farming, forestry, fishing, manufacturing, construction, and mining) employed more than 80 percent of workers in 1850, while services employed a bit fewer than 20 percent; today, those figures are almost completely reversed. The crossover point was 1950, when employment was nearly evenly divided among the sectors.[18]

This change in employment has had profound implications in terms of wages and benefits (see Table 3.1). From 1979 to 1996, employment in the manufacturing sector dropped by 10 percent (from 22 to 19.7 million), as did wages (from $12.72 to $11.47 an hour, in 1996 dollars). Over the same period, employment in

Table 3.1

The Costs of the Shift from Manufacturing to Services

Sector	1979	1996	% change
Manufacturing			
Annual average employment (millions)	22.0	19.7	-10
Median hourly wage	$12.72	$11.47	-10
Services			
Annual average employment (millions)	58.3	83.8	+44
Median hourly wage	$10.39	$10.00	-4

Source: Stephen A. Herzenberg, John A. Alic, and Howard Wial, *New Rules for a New Economy: Employment and Opportunity in Postindustrial America*, A Twentieth Century Fund Book (Ithaca, N.Y.: Cornell University Press, 1998), pp. 23 and 27, Tables 3 and 4.

services rose some 44 percent (from 58.3 to 83.8 million), but wages in that sector dropped 4 percent (from $10.39 to $10.00 an hour, in 1996 dollars).[19]

The overall outcome of this shift in sectors is a drop in income as well as a loss of benefits. The loss of benefits is a result of the weakening of the manufacturing sector, where unions were much more prevalent and had the power and will to fight for them. Unfortunately, as manufacturing declined, so did union membership. According to the Federal Reserve Bank of Cleveland, union membership fell from a high of almost 35 percent of workers in 1954 to a little more than 15 percent in 1994.[20]

The services sector is an extremely complex entity in terms of workers' skills. Consequently, the average hourly wage can be somewhat misleading. The two largest groups within the sector are professional services, where people earn on average $11.53 an hour, and retail trade, where hourly wages average $6.50. Those displaced from manufacturing and even middle-management ranks tend not to have the skills to find employment in the highest-paid areas of the service sector.

Another problem is that jobs in the service sector change far more rapidly than those in manufacturing. For one thing, the service sector is knowledge, not equipment, based, which allows for far more experimentation and far easier implementation of technological changes than is possible in huge manufacturing plants. Linotype operators found themselves jobless when type could be set by anyone who could use a computer. Retraining was extremely difficult because linotype machines used a different keyboard. Moreover, typesetting on these new machines did not pay as well because it was a relatively easy skill to acquire. When the insurance industry computerized, many of the back-office operations that had been done by hand by row upon row of clerks who calculated payments, prepared invoices, and checked accounts were turned over to machines that could do the work of ten people with one operator. With further advances in technology, the industry found it could replace many of its sales agents who had been earning good commissions with low-paid customer service representatives sitting in front of computers that presented them with scripted conversations allowing them to sell policies to customers who called in with questions.

Another change brought by the shift to the service sector was in the size of the companies for which most people worked. Manufacturing requires such huge investments in plant and equipment that companies engaged in that sector tend to be immense. Service-sector companies tend to be smaller. According to the Small Business Administration, between 1991 and 1995 companies that employed more than five hundred workers eliminated more than three million jobs, while companies employing fewer than five hundred employees created almost eleven million jobs (more than seven million of them with companies that employed fewer than nineteen people, and slightly more than half of those were in companies that employed from one to four workers). Start-ups have increased even more dramatically since then, which accounts for a large portion of the recent dramatic fall in unemployment rates.[21] Although these companies have created many new jobs, it is important to remember the downside of employment by smaller companies: they usually offer fewer benefits. Moreover, the smaller the company, the greater the risks that it will not survive over the long term.

Feeling the Pain

Once corporations learned how to make them operate efficiently, these new organizational models proved successful for the general economy, for shareholders, and for CEOs. Those who paid the price for this revitalization of the American corporation were the employees. In the current strong economy, there is work for everyone with skills. Indeed, the startling numbers of displaced workers are usually matched by equally startling numbers of jobs created in the same period. The problem, however, is that the nature of the skills in demand keeps changing. It is now normal for the same companies that open their front doors to workers with the skills they need to escort out their back doors workers whose skills have become obsolete. Many of today's workers—the so-called knowledge workers of our new world of information and services—have been through these revolving doors more than once, leaving them uncertain and angry.

- In 1996, AT&T eliminated 7,700 jobs, but their workforce at the end of the year was the same size as twelve months earlier because they hired so many workers for jobs that were created as they moved into new areas of business.[22]

- In 1995, 17 percent of the five million contingent workers in the United States were working for companies they had worked for before; 30 percent of companies that downsized in 1996 brought back downsized workers in a different role.[23]

The anxiety provoked by these actions was felt by everyone—even those who were never downsized—for a number of reasons. First, the magnitude of the downsizings was so enormous that nearly everyone knew someone—a relative, friend, or neighbor—who had lost a job or worked in an organization that had downsized. Second, the downsizings were managed in a way that often intensified the dismay of everyone involved. Third, the media focus on this issue was intense, in part because it affected the middle class—people just like them. And fourth, it was impossible not to notice—and resent—Wall Street's encouragement of such actions. Every announcement of cuts seemed to be greeted with approbation in the form of increased stock value.

It's Not What You Do, It's How You Do It

The ways in which companies handled downsizing were, and to a large extent remain, the problem. While some companies developed programs that took into account that they were breaking an implied social contract (see Box 3.2), most did not. Repeated downsizings in the absence of personal communications about what was taking place created the most resentment.

For example, in the summer of 1991, forty-five-year-old J. Thomas Byrom of San Francisco was earning $117,000 as senior vice president in charge of branch analysis at First Nationwide Bank. An MBA graduate from Stanford University, Byrom had been a banker for eighteen years. One morning he walked into his office and found a separation package on his desk that said he was

Box 3.2
Central and South West Corporation

Central and South West Corporation (CSW), a major public utility holding company in the Southwest, restructured in the face of deregulation in 1992. As they explored the issues involved in changing the organization to move from a protected monopoly to a newly competitive environment, senior management realized that they would have to modernize operations and acquire people with new skills—not just at this time but in all likelihood again and again in the future.

E. Richard Brooks, chairman of the board, president, and chief executive officer of CSW, said that contemplating this reorganization, which would mean reducing their workforce, compelled them to face the fact that many people who worked for a utility believed they had made certain trade-offs in return for job security. Brooks said that the retrenchment had "broken an unwritten pact—full lifetime employment." He explained that before they took this action, management spent a great deal of time working out a severance arrangement. Looking back at the decision-making process, he added that his employees "were responsible for our success," and asked, "how could we just let them go?"

Brooks and his management team decided to establish an employee task force to make recommendations on how the reorganization should be handled; the recommendations were, for the most part, accepted. Moreover, the task force's involvement helped bring acceptance of the decisions among those who remained: they knew it wasn't just those in charge—those who had the large salaries, who didn't understand "real life"—who had made the decisions.

The result was a $100 million package that involved early retirement, a continuation of benefits, up to eighteen months of financing for retraining for those who were not of retirement age, and a reduction of some 1,100 employees, about 12 percent of the workforce. Although the announcement of these actions had an adverse effect on share price, the company maintained its unbroken forty-three-year record of dividend increases. The goal behind such a costly decision was to send a message that the company was still a good place to work.

CSW's leadership also announced that in the future they would emphasize education and training for all employees, which, they believed, would make it possible to realize the many changes that may be called for in the future. The result was clear when it came to company morale and image. After the downsizing had taken place, when a CSW employee won over $19 million as his share of the Texas lottery, he explained to reporters that he wasn't going to quit: "Work is a priority in my life, and CSW is like my family."

Source: Based on author interviews, this material is adapted from John G. Sifonis and Beverly Goldberg, *Corporation on a Tightrope: Balancing Leadership, Governance, and Technology in an Age of Complexity* (New York: Oxford University Press, 1996), pp. 67–68.

entitled to three-and-a-half-months' severance. After a few months of fruitless searching, he decided to make a new start. Byrom began selling insurance on commission, and his wife started a business raising herbs in the garden of their 2.4-acre home, hoping to bring in an extra $10,000 to $15,000 a year.[24]

In 1993, when Tom Brown was forty-four, McKesson, a large wholesale drug distributor for which he'd worked for thirteen years as comptroller for the New York region, gave him notice. He says that though he knew that layoffs were inevitable, he did not expect the treatment he received. "Management didn't want to talk to me after my position had been eliminated," he says. "They basically didn't want to know that I existed."[25]

In January 1994, fifty-one-year-old Robert Gusciora, who had been an electrical engineer with Xerox for almost thirty years, found himself unemployed. "Losing my job," he said, "was the most shocking experience I've ever had in my life. I almost think it's worse than the death of a loved one, because at least we learn about death as we grow up. No one in my age group ever learned about being laid off."[26]

Countless other stories, many far worse than those related here, are commonplace. Some companies, worried about protecting files and data, called workers to meeting rooms in groups and dismissed them. Instead of allowing them to return to their offices after the meetings, they escorted them to other parts of the building, or in the case of the technology division of a large northeastern insurance company, to another site altogether. Once there, they were told to turn in their badges, were handed termination packages, and were given the personal belongings from their offices and the contents of their desks, neatly boxed. Although they received generous severance and outplacement services, the damage was severe. Still other companies tried to push people to leave on their own (see Box 3.3).

Media Empathy

The anxiety created by being downsized or watching it happen to others was exacerbated by the intense media coverage of the problem. Not only did the media recount the stories of pain experienced by the downsized but they seemed to focus on plans for downsizing. In the latter case, the media performed a public service: Publicly held corporations are obligated to announce downsizings in

Box 3.3
AT&T

Working for AT&T over the past decade was a lot like running with the bulls: nobody knew if and when they would get gored. Employees first had to figure out what it meant for them when CEO Robert E. Allen said he was cutting forty thousand jobs, and then when new CEO C. Michael Armstrong announced he was cutting an additional fifteen thousand to eighteen thousand positions. Would they find another job in the company before the sixty days they were given to do so ran out? If they did, should they relocate to take it? And if they took it, would the new job be eliminated in the next round, leaving them not only without a job but without a support network of close family and friends nearby? What kind of "voluntary retirement package" should they grab? When was the time right to accept such an offer?

Ever since the breakup of the Bell System, AT&T has changed from the perfect place to work—for white-collar employees who could anticipate lifetime employment with the regulated monopoly—to a model of the new world of work. From the breakup of Ma Bell in 1984 to 1995, 120,000 jobs were cut. In 1995, Allen announced that it would take slashing the payroll to renew the company. Then early in 1996, he finally announced that the renewal would take 40,000 cuts by the end of the year. Within months of that announcement, Allen received a record compensation package, including salary and bonus of $2.7 million and a huge package of stock options. Even though the downsizing he planned never came close to the numbers he had announced, the psychological damage to workers was immense. And the trauma did not end there. In 1998, new CEO Michael Armstrong achieved his goal of cutting

18,000 jobs. This latest effort is paying off—at least for shareholders. AT&T stock reached an all-time high early in January 1999.

The costs to AT&T's workers—those who lost their jobs as well as those who managed to find new positions within the company and those whose jobs were never threatened—has been enormous. At AT&T, workers are not told they are fired, given a severance package, then depart shortly afterward. First come the public announcements about plans to downsize. Then, after everyone has time to speculate on what this will mean to him or her and who might be competing for the positions that will remain, comes notification that all are "at risk" and "available for reassignment," that one's job has become "surplus." During this stage, people are left to their own devices. They call everyone they know in the company trying to find a position within the sixty days allotted to that activity. If they find something that requires relocation, they have to decide whether they think that job will last.

At higher levels, there are offers of voluntary early retirement packages. Deciding whether enough other employees will opt out to make your job safe or whether to grab the package if you are among those eligible is the next game played. In this latest round, leaving proved easy for the eligibles. Not only was the package generous, but for those not ready to give up working, new jobs were not that hard to find in a booming economy.

What has proved most difficult for AT&T employees to accept is the constant uncertainty, the knowledge that this is not the last round of disruptions. The road back has been very difficult for many. The stories of how they coped with the unraveling of a seemingly ideal American workplace have been thoroughly covered in countless articles and an in-depth study of six survivors of these events by Barbara

Rudolph. Their experiences stand as a model of the personal costs incurred by all those living through the pain caused by the remaking of the world of work.

Sources: Barbara Rudolph, *Disconnected: How Six People from AT&T Discovered the New Meaning of Work in a Downsized Corporate America* (New York: Free Press, 1998); Brian O'Reilly, "Ma Bell's Orphans," *Fortune*, April 1, 1996; Peter Elstrom, "Mike Armstrong's Strong Showing," *Business Week*, January 25, 1999; various stories in the business press.

advance because such actions qualify as significant events that may affect their stock price; not announcing such things as the costs of future severance liabilities and restructuring could open executives to charges involving the use of insider information.

The media's concentration on the plight of those who thought they had made it to a comfortable life and then found themselves suffering emotionally as well as financially had different roots. The media had not ignored such events in the past, but reports of layoffs in manufacturing, particularly in automobile manufacturing, were usually mitigated by statements about the supplements the unions were providing those laid off to help replace salary and the scope of the benefits, such as health insurance, that would continue to be paid as a result of the contracts the unions negotiated. Moreover, in many fields layoffs were not considered news because the work was seasonal or jobs were low-level enough to be replaced easily by other kinds of work. In addition, those in lower-paid jobs were not in the same danger of losing expensive homes.

Unemployment among higher-paid managerial employees created problems for banks with large stocks of housing that few could afford. The neighborhoods and communities that were supported by the taxes those workers had been paying also encountered many problems. In fact, unemployment among middle managers had serious financial ramifications for the economy as a whole.

These stories of the downsizings of middle managers also had strong human interest appeal, in part because so many of those affected turned out to be articulate spokespersons for this new class of unemployed. The media were quick to cover stories of downsized workers, such as those who still hadn't told their spouses what had happened and thus were leaving home every morning as if they were going to work. These people had worked for firms such as IBM and Kodak, the very companies that were at the heart of the myth of lifetime employment. As a result, their employees felt secure and comfortable and had no experience dealing with more uncertainty than the size of their next raise. Nothing had prepared them for this new world of work.

The major reason for the intense, detailed, constant coverage, however, was much more personal. Those reporting on this issue empathized with the middle managers being downsized. Observers of this phenomenon noted that reporters, "especially business journalists, report *about* and *for* the top strata of the occupational ladder. . . . [They] pay disproportionate attention to downsizing toward the top rungs of the occupational hierarchy because these workers are disproportionately their friends and relatives and readers and listeners."[27]

Wall Street Rewards

The way downsizing was handled and the way it was reported weren't the only reasons for the bitterness. The displaced and downsized were in pain, and they quickly began to resent the companies to which they had devoted so much time and effort. What made the process even more difficult to endure psychologically was that the mere announcement of an impending downsizing brought ailing companies an immediate return—a return on disinvesting in employees. To workers, it often seemed as if the message was "workers do not add value." On the day in late 1993 that the Xerox Corporation announced plans to cut its workforce by ten thousand workers, its stock rose 7 percent.[28]

Moreover, this road to change has come to be a habit. Hedrick Smith, a former reporter for the *New York Times,* summed up this addiction to downsizing by explaining that "downsizing is like dieting: everyone is doing it, so people try it again and again, even though few have achieved the desired results. As one wag put it, the fixation with downsizing has become the new 'corporate anorexia.' "[29]

The real problem with this corporate dieting is that those affected by it take a long time to find new work, and the work they find usually does not restore them to their previous earnings level. They also lose because while searching they dip into savings, which were often meant for retirement, to maintain their lifestyles—or just to survive. Those who escape the downsizings also suffer. They experience guilt, fear, resentment, overwork, and constant uncertainty.

It sometimes seems that the only winners are high-paid CEOs and stockholders. Stock ownership may provide some of the answers to the question, Why have people accepted all this with so little protest? Today, with mutual funds and pensions invested in the market, more and more people feel that everyone gains from corporate successes in the long run. In addition, it is hard to gear up for a fight when the economy is strong and jobs go begging for lack of skilled labor. People begin to believe that if somehow they had just worked harder or acquired some additional skills, they wouldn't be on the losing side.

The Tough New World of Work

The changes that have marked the world of work over the past two decades have brought about both a strong economy and a shortage of workers. The world of work is now a churning sea of constant change, new skills, new mergers and acquisitions. Global competition has led to still more turmoil. In December 1998, Boeing announced it would lay off as many as 38,000 workers by the end of 1999 because of the economic downturn in Asia; Johnson & Johnson announced it would cut some 4,100 jobs over the next twelve to eighteen months in a restructuring; and Mobil and Exxon were expected to downsize by at least 20,000 as a result of their merger.

However, even though Americans recognize that what happens in one area of the globe affects business in every other area, and that rapid technological advances demand new skills, they still want employers to accept some responsibility toward those who work for them. There is an underlying belief that something is morally and ethically wrong with a workplace that creates so much stress and anxiety that employees just don't care and seek to escape from work, especially work for large organizations.

Chapter 4

The Race to Retirement

"I can't wait to retire ... no pressure ... my time my own. I want a place in the sun, where I can read and relax and not worry ... about learning another new program, meeting another set of crazy deadlines. I can't wait till all I have to do is what I want to do."

"There's just not enough time now. I spend endless hours at work so I won't get let go if they downsize again. I can't wait to retire ... then I'll travel, volunteer, maybe start a small business, even learn a foreign language."

"My dad retired at sixty and he says he's having a great time. He never earned as much as I do—he worked in a factory all his life. I think I want to retire early, the way he did. I don't know though if I want to just do nothing ... but I really hate going into the office lately."

The combination of disillusionment with the workplace and the anticipated pleasures of early retirement reflected in these comments bodes ill for the future of corporate America. Yet the comments do not indicate so much a desire not to work at all but, rather, a desire to escape from stressful and unpleasant jobs and companies that are neither liked nor trusted. Indeed, more and more evidence is emerging that the boomers' concept of retirement is very different from that of their parents. Boomers indicate that they plan to spend part of their retirement working at least part-time. Unfortunately, these new perceptions of retirement and current corporate policies and actions do not mesh. Corporations must develop a greater understanding of the boomers' newly emerging vision of retirement and then adjust their organizational structures to accommodate it now. Only by doing so can they create a workplace that will allow them to retain their present workforce as well as recruit an adequate workforce for the future.

Life in the Third Age

When the first boomers, those born after 1946, were ready to enter the workforce in the mid- to late 1960s, there weren't enough jobs to go around; this situation worsened as more of that huge generation began to enter the workforce. As a result, older workers were encouraged to retire to make jobs available for these younger workers.

From a business perspective, workers retiring early provided a number of benefits. First, it reduced salaries. A large number of Americans were employed in manufacturing at the time, and older employees earned far more than their replacements would because of the strength of unions and the seniority system. Another advantage of retirement was that the younger people entering the workforce would provide a new generation of consumers. They would be setting up their own households and having families. (No one expected the boomers to put off having children as long as they did, or to have so few of them.) Moreover, many hoped that new markets would be created by retirees trading in one lifestyle for another, an expectation that was soon realized. For policymakers, the retirement of older workers solved the problem of having a huge group of unemployed and underemployed young people unhappily awaiting their chance to build a life.

This push to hasten retirement was welcomed by a generation that had lived through the Depression and a world war; most had spent long years at relatively hard physical work. The acceptance of retirement as a period of leisure, a chance to do the things they had never had the time or money to do while raising their families, was aided by the way Social Security had been sold to the public as an insurance program, something that they had earned.

Retirement rapidly became idealized as the golden years, a stress-free stage of life, a time for relaxation or travel. It was the third stage of life, supported in part by good pensions from the companies for which employees had worked for decades and in part by Social Security benefits, which were higher than recipients ever dreamed possible because of the strong economy and America's interest in social progress in the postwar years. In addition, these retirees were eligible for Medicare, enacted in 1965 to protect them from the most frightening expense of old age—health care costs. And for many, there was also the money from selling the house they had bought after the war and now owned outright, which allowed them to purchase a retirement home and put aside funds for pleasure.

Many retirees bought homes in new communities built specifically for them in comfortable, sunny climates. These communities of older people were safe from the urban turmoil becoming all too prevalent in the late 1970s. Dora Costa reports in *The Evolution of Retirement* that retirees "sharply increased time spent on their favorite hobbies or recreational activities." For example, people reported traveling three times more often after they retired than before, taking vacations running the gamut from trips abroad to touring the states in their campers.[1] Even those with limited income could enjoy their leisure more than past retires, as the availability of low-cost recreational activities increased through advances in technology (from the development of video cassette machines to cable television) and the development of countless publicly and privately supported programs aimed at seniors.

During the last quarter of the twentieth century, retirement became a norm rather than an exception. As more people retired at sixty-five, and some started retiring even earlier, it began to seem the natural thing to do. The movement to earlier retirement gained momentum during the last decade of the century as downsized workers who could not find jobs decided to retire permanently, ending their fruitless job searches.

The normalization of retirement was aided by the coverage of retirement by the media. The stories in the media tended to be extremely positive. The media did not seem to be overly attracted to reporting on the feelings of people in these retirement communities as they grew older and became less active. Many became uncomfortable with the isolation from the young and from their families, especially as they entered their late seventies. They felt trapped in a place where they waited until morning to see who the ambulance had come for at 2 A.M. Little is heard about those who are depressed by not being needed, making no difference, and living a life that seems never to vary.

Build It and They Will Come

The acceptance of retirement as a new norm is most evident in the labor force participation rates of men. In 1950, almost half of men over sixty-five were still in the labor force; by 1970, a little over a quarter were; by 1990 only 16.4 percent worked. The trend toward earlier retirement is most evident in the period from 1970 to 1990, when labor force participation rates of men fell from 83.0 percent to 67.7 percent.

- The average age of retirement has declined steadily, dropping from 67 in 1950 to 62.7 in 1995.
- Even the labor force participation rates of men fifty-five to sixty-four dropped—from 86.9 percent in 1950 to 66.0 percent in 1995.

The choice of early retirement may have become a norm, but it also begs a number of questions. What is an appropriate age for retirement? What financial issues are involved? Is full retirement really what people want? If not, what are the alternatives to standard retirement and what would it take to change people's minds about when and how to retire? Because the retirement decisions of the boomers will have such a large impact on all our futures, we need to find the answers to these questions.

Why Sixty-Five?

One of the questions that arises when studying the subject of retirement is, Why is sixty-five considered the right age for retirement? Although there has been a worldwide trend toward earlier retirement and some people still say that they never want to retire, the age around which these decisions revolve is sixty-five.

Traditionally, Social Security and most pension plans have been structured to begin paying out benefits in full at sixty-five. Indeed, state legislatures set sixty-five as the proper age for retirement in constructing their pension systems well before the passage of Social Security in 1935. Was this date chosen because something happens to us at sixty-five?

In *Age Wave*, Ken Dychtwald's book that looks at the aging of the population in 1990, he explains that the choice of sixty-five as the age for retirement has its origins in demographics. When German chancellor Otto von Bismarck established the first state social security system in 1889, he set the retirement age at seventy—the biblical life span of three score and ten. Doing so allowed Bismarck to offer a popular social boon at little cost, since he was advised that almost no one lived to that age. German life expectancy in 1889 was forty-five, which meant that the retirement age of seventy was 56 percent higher than the life expectancy rate.[2]

When Social Security legislation was enacted in the United States in the mid-1930s, the average life expectancy was sixty-one years and seven months; those over sixty-five constituted less than 7 percent of the population and could expect to live about twelve years past retirement. Those responsible for determining when people should retire chose sixty-five as the right age based on probable cost and comparability with similar plans in European nations (Germany's retirement age had been lowered to sixty-five some time earlier). In his 1999 book *Gray Dawn,* Peter Peterson points out that if the normal age of retirement when Social Security was put in place "had been 'indexed' to longevity since 1935, today's workers would be waiting to 73 to receive full benefits."[3]

For most of the past century, there was considerable support for making sixty-five the age for retirement. In 1916, Isaac Rubinow, a social scientist, wrote that "Age 65 is generally set as the threshold of old age since it is at this period of life that the rates for sickness and death begin to show a marked increase over those of earlier years." In 1980, the federal government argued in a case about the constitutionality of the Railroad Retirement Act before the Supreme Court: "It is a commonplace fact that physical ability, mental alertness, and cooperativeness tend to fail after a man is 65."[4]

If the age for retirement were being set today using the same criteria, the year selected would, in all likelihood, be dramatically different. The following facts would have to be considered in setting a new age for retirement:

- The proportion of the U.S. population over sixty-five is projected to reach 13 percent in 2000, double what it was when the retirement age was set at sixty-five in 1935; it will reach 21.8 percent in 2050.

- The number of the oldest old (those over eight-five) was 3.5 million in 1994; it is expected to double to 7 million by 2020.
- From 1982 to 1994, chronic disability declined by 15 percent for the U.S. population over age sixty-five.[5]

In light of how much longer people are living and how much healthier they are when older, should the standard age of retirement be changed? The first step has already been taken to push people to stay in the workforce longer: As part of the last round of legislation aimed at ensuring the future solvency of the Social Security system, the age for collecting full Social Security benefits was increased on a sliding scale for future retirees—to sixty-seven for those born in 1960 or later.

Where Will the Money Come From?

Although many people look forward to retirement, even hoping and planning to retire early, few seem to have done the math necessary to determine what it will take to finance their retirement. Most individuals seem reluctant to face the reality of building a financial position that will allow them to achieve a comfortable retirement, perhaps because they do not want to face their own aging or because they don't believe they can save what it may take.

One of the first issues to examine is how long retirement will be. Now that people live much longer, they must plan for many years spent in retirement. Moreover, using the figures for life expectancy at birth is a mistake, because the closer to retirement, the longer life expectancy is. Someone who is already sixty-five is likely to spend more than a dozen years in retirement (see Figure 1.4).

It also is important to keep in mind that different stages of retirement require different amounts of income. When younger and more vigorous, retirees spend more money on travel and entertainment than they do in the later years of retirement. At the same time, those later years raise the specter of long-term medical care or the need for assisted living, which is extremely expensive. (The government does not provide assistance in such cases except for the destitute.) Of course, there are ways to achieve a happy, comfortable retirement without a lot of money. For example, many seniors enjoy volunteer work, which provides companionship, a sense of identity and belonging, as well as the satisfaction that comes from giving of one's self. For others, television and community center activities may be enough to provide a satisfactory lifestyle as they become older. Once retirees determine the level of income they will want, accumulating the needed resources is the issue.

Most people depend on a three-legged stool for their retirement income: Social Security, pensions, and savings. Social Security is likely to remain the most solid leg of the retirement stool in spite of the problems the system seemed to be facing until the economic boom of the late 1990s. Although the doomsayers were proclaiming that the system would collapse under the weight of all those boomer retirees and Generation X would never receive Social Security at all, the truth was that even if, as projected, the Social Security Trust Funds were depleted in 2023—and no changes were made—retirees from that date forward still would have received 75 percent of the payments owed them. The reason is simple: Social Security is a pay-as-you-go system, which means current payroll taxes are used to pay current retirees. The payroll taxes on the workforce of 2023 would cover three-quarters of the amount owed retirees in that year.

The Social Security Trust Funds were set up to supplement the funds collected from the payroll tax and thus solve the potential problem of the shortfalls that the retirement of the boomers would cause. In fact the amount in the funds had grown enough to cover the first dozen years after the boomers begin retiring. Thus the problem really was finding a way to make up the missing 25 per-

cent after 2023. The doomsayers were ignoring that the anticipated shortfall in the Trust Funds was based on projections that
the average annual increase in U.S. gross domestic product would
be 1.6 percent, adjusted for inflation, from 1997 to 2027. This
projected growth rate was even lower than the actual growth rate
in the difficult years 1975–96, when it averaged 2.7 percent.[6] In
1999, gross domestic product was averaging 4 percent, and the
government was debating what to do with its unanticipated sur-
pluses.

The uproar over the system was created in large part by a report of the Social Security trustees, who are charged with project-
ing the performance of the system over a seventy-five-year time
horizon, using very modest assumptions. This procedure is a
means of alerting the government to possible future problems
early enough for preventive action to be taken. However, the
problems facing Social Security proved far less serious than anticipated by those who proclaimed the imminent collapse of the system unless dramatic measures were taken.

When it comes to the second leg of the stool, employer-provided
pensions, the situation is somewhat shakier. More than half of
Americans working in the private sector—some fifty-one million individuals—are not covered by a retirement plan provided by their
employer. In addition, each year five million of those who are covered change jobs, losing their pension benefits.[7]

Another reason employer-provided pensions no longer provide
as solid a base is the change in the nature of those pensions from
defined benefit plans to defined contribution plans. As Brookings
Institution economist William G. Gale explains, "In defined benefit
plans, annuity benefits are stipulated as a percentage of years
worked, average or maximum salaries, and other considerations.
In defined contribution plans, employees typically have much more
control over not only whether to participate but also how much to
contribute, where to invest, and how and when to withdraw funds.
All of these options raise concerns about the adequacy of retirement saving."[8] Thus, the problem with the defined contribution

plans are the added risk as well as the optional employee contributions—Americans tend to be shortsighted about putting aside money for the future.

There is, however, another side to this issue. Defined contribution plans do not require staying with a single company for any specific length of time. In this new environment in which companies downsize, restructure, and merge frequently, Ian Farman of William M. Mercer, a pension and benefits company, says that these plans make more sense. They are "a backpack pension that individuals can carry around with them through life." You do not lose your pension because you weren't with a company long enough for the money in the pension fund to vest.[9]

The third leg of the stool, personal savings (as a percentage of disposable personal income), presents very different problems from the other two. People are responsible for providing their own savings, and to date, people have not been very successful at saving. At the same time, in the current economic climate, although the personal savings rate in the United States is low—under 2 percent for the first two quarters of 1998[10]—investment in the stock market through mutual funds has become fairly common. Given the market performance of the past few years, this may mean that the failure to save for retirement is less important, but as the market fluctuations of the second half of 1998 showed, investing in stocks is never a sure thing.

Some baby boomers are counting on inheritances from their parents as at least a partial solution to the problem of financing their retirement. For most people, however, inheritances are not likely to prove a reliable source of retirement income. Although Mom and Pop may have had a big house that they sold for a substantial sum, as Laurence Kotlikoff points out in *Generational Accounting*, the parents of the baby boomers are "retiring earlier and living longer, and therefore, consuming more of their bequeathable wealth." He also points out that most of the financial assets of boomers' parents will disappear when they die because it is in the form of pensions and Social Security.[11] In addition, boomers are part of larger families (remember, the average fertility rate hovered well over three during the baby boom, which means three or four siblings per boomer when those without any children are factored out). A group of three surviving siblings means three adult children will be around to share any inheritance. Indeed, the average inheritance of baby boomers is likely to be in the $10,000 to $30,000 range, a drop in the bucket when it comes to their retirement needs.[12]

In general, the Employee Benefit Research Institute (EBRI) in Washington, D.C., which conducted a Retirement Confidence Survey in 1997, says that Americans are not preparing very well for retirement. Although 63 percent of Americans report that they have begun to save for retirement, only 45 percent have tried to figure out how much they will need to save. The same survey showed that 34 percent of preretirees and 35 percent of older boomers were not very confident about their ability to maintain a comfortable lifestyle after retirement, while only 28 percent of younger boomers and 24 percent of Generation Xers had the same qualms. Moreover, 32 percent of Generation Xers were very confident that they would have comfortable retirements.[13] Those numbers reflect that for most people, the closer retirement draws, the more they doubt they actually will have enough money to be comfortable once they do retire. It is a case of reality bites—the realization that the future for which they meant to save is here and they haven't done so.

In fact, if reality bites as late as it usually does, and if history is any indication, retirees are likely to face major problems in the future. Although the late 1990s were marked by low inflation, the EBRI reports that even among those "early retirees who reported that they could afford to retire early, 30 percent have seen their standard of living decline since they retired, and 36 percent are now not confident that they will have enough money to remain comfortable throughout retirement."[14]

The message is clear. In deciding when to retire, individuals will have to balance the probability of longer life after retirement and the possibility of inflation against the amount they have accumulated in savings and pensions to determine whether it makes sense to continue to work, even if only part-time, particularly in their earlier retirement years while they are more fit and their skills still have some relevance.

Redefining the Future

Retirement decisions are based on more than economics. For those prudent, or lucky, enough to afford to retire when they choose, there are other issues to resolve. First, retirees must decide whether or not their sense of self is wrapped up in their work. Will they find it enough to answer the question, "What do you do?" with "I used to be . . ."? Do they depend on colleagues for friendship? Are they easily bored when not learning something new and facing new challenges?

Of course, remaining active does not require remaining at work. Pursuing studies in an area of interest or doing more with a hobby can provide continued intellectual stimulation. Working for an environmental group, joining a political party, or even standing for the local school board or town council can meet the need for identity. Working with children, the elderly, animals, or the poor can provide a sense of great fulfillment.

Then retirees must decide if they really have saved enough for retirement. Many retirees quickly discover that they may not have enough for a prolonged retirement. These retirees need to find a way to supplement their retirement income. Returning to work poses a number of challenges, including a lack of up-to-date skills, age discrimination, and the loss of Social Security income after earning a certain amount, which makes full-time employment costly—if it is even available.

Another group includes retirees who just enjoy working and would prefer not to leave the workforce but do not want to work full-time. In this group are those who retired from jobs they hated and who now want to work at something new, different, and less stressful and those who want to work for themselves.

These people are becoming part of a large group now referred to as the working retired. Although "retirement has been promoted as such a desirable goal in maturity that fully 70 percent of working-age Americans believe that a comfortable retirement is a fundamental part of the American dream," according to Ken Dychtwald in his latest book, *Age Power,* surveys indicate that the meaning of retirement is changing to include working after retirement.[15] The future of this new model of work, however, is uncertain.

Creating New Norms

While some experts are predicting that the boomers will redefine retirement, just as they have redefined every other stage of life as they entered it, the boomers cannot change the face of retirement by sheer force of will. The history of social change shows that more is needed. In the past, national views of work have been driven by necessity and public opinion, and have changed in response to larger social needs. Marketing experts Philip Kotler and Eduardo Roberto explain social change as "an organized effort conducted by one group (the change agent), which intends to persuade others (the target adopters) to accept, modify, or abandon certain ideas, attitudes, practices, and behavior."[16]

For example, the way people thought about women's role in the workforce changed as a result of a social change campaign during World War II. Before the war, women were a very small part of the workforce and relegated, for the most part, to jobs with low status that did not pay well. Women, especially married women, were not welcome in the workplace. As soon as America entered the war, however, the problem arose of how to support a large military endeavor when the men who worked in the factories that could supply war materials were drafted and sent abroad. The response was to encourage women, in the name of patriotism, to join the ranks of workers in once all-male jobs, becoming shipbuilders and bus drivers, journalists and police officers, statisticians and ball players. Initially, businesses resisted this change despite their desperate need for workers, and the government had to develop a campaign to encourage companies to accept it. This campaign included films and spokespeople who promoted the acceptability of women working, even doing demanding physical labor. Newspaper articles praised those women, especially married women with husbands in the military, and magazines featured them as heroines.

The effort succeeded: Eighteen million women joined the workforce in civilian and defense jobs. Then the war ended, and the men started coming home. The need to find work for these veterans became a major concern, and pink slips were handed out, forcing women to return to the home. The propaganda machine, aided by American business, once again swung into high gear. These women, many of whom had worked in challenging jobs for a number of years, were once again encouraged to accept the role of homemaker.[17] America became a nation of stay-at-home wives and mothers and hardworking men trying to advance up the career ladder and provide their children, the baby boomers, with the good life.

This second round of social change did not achieve a complete reversal in the workforce participation of women. Moreover, as a result of women's participation in the workforce, the idea that they could achieve success in many different fields was no longer unthinkable.[18] In fact, the experiences of women who worked during the war influenced the way they raised their daughters. These women wanted more education and independence for their daughters. Those attitudes had unexpected and far-reaching consequences. The far-better-educated women of the baby boom did not embrace marriage, home, and childbearing with the enthusiasm their mothers had—at least not until they had explored life and their own abilities a lot longer. Thus, the first unexpected consequence of the propaganda aimed at getting women to work was the baby boom itself as the active and enthusiastic workers of World War II returned home and began to have families; the second was the entry of large numbers of women into the workforce; and the third was the baby bust caused by the liberated attitudes and ambitions of this new generation of working women.

One of the important lessons to draw from these events is that what people accept as reasonable behavior is based almost entirely on the social norms of a given era. It often takes something dramatic, in this case war, to make them reexamine that behavior. At that point, social change efforts can begin. Thus, if American business offers more flexible arrangements, it may attract much needed workers who won't accept full-time work, and make working retired the new norm.

The First Changes

The major changes that have taken place in the images of retirement reflect the improved health of older people, the need to be involved, the drive to learn and explore, and the financial and social attractions of work.

LIVING STRONGER

Today, retirees do not limit their participation in sports to a few laps in the pool and a nine-hole game of golf. Senior olympics, senior track-and-field events, swim meets, and ninety-three-year-olds in the New York City Marathon are all part of the lifestyles pursued by those once considered over the hill. The technological advances that changed the world of work also had a huge impact on medicine. New knees and heart valves have made it possible for seniors to remain active well into their retirement years. Bessie Goldberg, who works in the volunteer office of a Staten Island hospital putting her old bookkeeping skills to good use and who helps raise funds for the Staten Island Senior Olympics, had to give up race walking in her mid-seventies, but that didn't stop her from joining the senior cheerleading squad. Local gyms have special classes for older citizens, and finding older members who spend a few hours a week weight training is not difficult.

Travel for seniors no longer means bus tours of museums in nearby states. Many of today's seniors vacation by white-water rafting in the Grand Canyon and biking tours in China and India. For example, Nadine Heyman, a retired Long Island school principal, took a jeep trip through the Baliem Valley in Indonesia with a group of fifty-plus adventurers in 1998 at the age of sixty-five. Gene Wellman, a retired environmental consultant from Oregon, traveled through Peru and French Polynesia at seventy-one.[19]

Now that so many baby boomers have made the pursuit of fitness a part of their lifestyles, the attraction of these activities is likely to increase. The implications of this for the workplace are enormous. After all, one of the reasons businesses have hesitated to employ older workers is their perception that older workers are neither strong nor healthy enough to keep working.

LENDING A HELPING HAND

The growth in the number of senior volunteers over the past two decades also provides insights into the new directions in which retirement may be headed. Organizations that turned to older volunteers when women entered the workforce in large numbers found that they were able to fill even the most demanding jobs. In some cases retirees end up doing the same work they once did for pay. For example, Emily Vallelong, an administrative director of volunteers at Sisters of Charity Medical Center/St. Vincent's Campus in Staten Island, says that many of the employees who retired from the hospital have come back as volunteers after a few weeks of leisure. Many even do the same jobs they did before retiring. These volunteers come back, according to Vallelong, because "they want to stay involved" and feel when volunteering that "they are in control," and they want to maintain the relationships that they have established over the years.[20]

Former President Jimmy Carter, who has now spent almost a quarter of a century both leading volunteer causes and doing hands-on volunteer work, sums up the views of retirees who devote countless hours to volunteer activities: "All these projects have enriched my life in untold ways. . . . While reaching out to others, Rosalynn and I have filled our own needs to be challenged and to act as productive members of the global community."[21]

GROWING WISER

Many university towns have become attractive places to settle for older Americans who want to keep learning. According to the Department of Education, 356,000 people between the ages of fifty and sixty-four were full- or part-time students pursuing degrees in 1998; another 80,000 plus were over sixty-five. For example, in 1998, Harry Gold, then seventy-four years old, received a degree in American history from Long Island University. Gold, who says he found exams "a real chore," not only graduated but his grade point average was 3.8.[22]

In addition, more than 60,000 retirees attend the almost three hundred colleges in forty-five states that offer academic, nondegree programs for retirees through Institutes for Learning in Retirement. These programs are so popular that applicants are screened before acceptance.[23] Moreover, an organization known as Elderhostel Inc. that offers courses to those over fifty-five at some two thousand locations had 263,000 enrollments in 1998.[24]

WORKING RETIRED

The most important development in terms of a possible redefinition of retirement is, as noted, the idea of working retired. It is a good way to describe those who consider themselves retired because they have withdrawn from steady work for a single organization, yet engage in some form of paid employment. In the past, most of those who could be defined as working retired were former policemen, firemen, teachers, or members of the military who retired after twenty to thirty years. Then, pension in hand, they went on to another career in their early forties or fifties.

Today, the working retired are far older, and they often find new approaches to the work they have always done. For example, John Wheeler of Albuquerque, a lawyer who once put in sixty-hour weeks, now works for himself, spending about thirty hours a week on his practice. Wheeler says, "I work when I want to. And that's my retirement or semiretirement. I don't think I'll ever really quit."[25]

Not only those in the professional world make these choices. According to the Bureau of Labor Statistics, more than 1.5 million people, including more than a hundred thousand over fifty-five, had turned to temporary placement agencies for employment by 1997. Anna Jeanne Flatten, a Minnesotan who left her office job in 1993 after thirteen years, decided she wanted to return to work four years later. At sixty-eight, finding full-time work proved impossible. So she listed with a temporary agency that specialized in placing seniors. Describing an eight-hour day she'd just put in, she said, "We have so much fun, and that's important."[26]

Stan Hinden, a retired financial writer for the *Washington Post*, writes a column for the paper called "Retirement Journal."

He voices similar sentiments: "Shortly after I retired from my job . . . I discovered something curious. I loved retirement. But I missed working. The contradiction was puzzling.

"I knew, of course, why I liked retirement; it gave me a wonderful sense of freedom. After 45 years of working, it was delightful to live by my own schedule. So, I asked myself, why do I miss working? . . . Eventually it dawned on me that what I missed most was not my work but my workplace. . . . The office had been my second home, a place where I could chat with friends, catch up on the gossip, swap rumors. . . . When I left the paper, I left all that behind."

Hinden explains that six months after he left the paper he came back to work part-time, writing a column on retirement. He says that the responses to his column indicate that he is far from alone in his desire to work retired.[27]

Pulling the Switch

Today's retirees are changing popular perceptions of retirement because they are healthy, vigorous, and want to remain active and do what brings them the most enjoyment. The reasons why corporations have not made concerted efforts to encourage older workers or to push this new vision of retirement are just as easy to find. Corporations have not adjusted to the possibilities of changing the nature of the workplace. Managers are wedded to a past in which the sound of the starting whistle at the factory meant that all workers had to be at their posts, where they would stay until the closing whistle blew. Today, most work is not done in factories; computer technology allows office work to be done across distance and time very easily, eliminating the need for people to work in close proximity. Does it matter that Joe and Sue in accounting each works half days entering figures on spreadsheets? Why does Bob have to drive through all that ice to get to the office when he can fax or e-mail his design to Barbara, who came into the office because she lives just down the street? Does it matter that telemarketers are retirees in the winter and students in the summer? Not really, and that view is slowly gaining a degree of acceptance. Yet there is something stronger at work in the corporate environment, an attitude that older is not only *not* better but that it is a problem.

Chapter 5

Attitudes and Assumptions

"We need young blood around here, the younger the better. We work crazy hours ... there's lots of stress."

"I've been trying to find a new job for over a year. Every time I walk in for an interview ... and there weren't many until I fixed my resume so you couldn't tell my age ... I can see 'that look.' Whoever is interviewing me keeps glancing at their watch. They want to be sure they give me that twenty minutes that means I can't claim they decided against me the minute they saw how old I am."

"We use the latest technology, sometimes switching programs every few months. So if people are older and aren't into technology, even if they know the current system, it's hard to get them to make a change."

The downsizings of the late 1980s and early 1990s destroyed the idea of organizational loyalty and created a general disillusionment with work. It also made the lure of retirement irresistible to many older workers. The increase in the exodus of workers over

104

fifty-five may have been dramatized by these forces, but its roots lie in the complex mix of attitudes toward and assumptions about older workers that long have resulted in discrimination against them and discomfort with their presence in the workplace.

Discrimination against older workers was prevalent even in the extraordinarily tight labor market of the late 1990s, when older workers had a far harder time finding new employment than their younger counterparts. In 1998, it took those aged fifty to sixty more than 65 percent longer to find a new job than it took someone thirty-five to forty; it took someone aged forty-six to fifty a little over 20 percent longer than it took a thirty-five year old.[1]

Employers have long believed that replacing older workers with younger ones is better for the bottom line and that younger workforces promote the image of organizations as growing, vibrant entities. These assumptions continue to hold sway. In fact, so long as there is a large pool of new entrants, companies are unlikely to change. While the tight labor markets at the close of the twentieth century did not change the minds of those wedded to the idea that younger is better, they did manage to awaken some human resources directors to the growing shortage of younger workers. If these directors take a leadership role in pointing out the need to make changes now, their organizations may be in a far stronger competitive position in ten years, when the workforce becomes even grayer (see Table 5.1).

As the baby boomers are replaced by the baby-bust generation, graying workers will become essential to our continued economic health. To ensure that the potential older workforce of tomorrow will be willing to participate in some capacity, companies must begin to explore and analyze age discrimination now. It is the only way to eliminate the attitudes and assumptions that cause it, driving so many older workers out and minimizing the contribution of so many others.

It is not fair, however, to place all the blame on employers. Age discrimination exists in the broader society as well as in the work-

Table 5.1

Percent of Population by Age, Working Years, 1995–2050

Year	18–24*	25–34	35–44	45–64
1995	9.4	15.5	16.1	19.8
2000	9.5	13.5	16.2	22.2
2005	9.8	12.6	14.7	24.8
2010	10.1	12.8	12.9	26.4
2020	9.2	13.3	12.2	24.6
2030	9.1	12.3	12.7	21.6
2040	9.3	12.4	11.9	21.9
2050	9.2	12.5	12.0	21.7

*A majority of those in this age group delay entering the workforce on a full-time basis until twenty-one or twenty-two to continue their education.

Source: Author's calculations from Jennifer Cheeseman Day, *Population Projections of the United States by Age, Sex, Race, and Hispanic Origins: 1995–2050* (U.S. Bureau of the Census, Current Population Reports, P25-1130, Washington, D.C.: Government Printing Office, 1996), p. 9, Table F.

place, and perhaps most difficult of all, older people share many of the attitudes and assumptions about age that are at the root of this form of discrimination. Sixty-year-old CEOs are as convinced of the need to hire younger workers to maintain or improve productivity and keep down costs as are forty-year-old managers.

Thus, the first step in dealing with this problem must be to discover the reasons behind the prejudice. To do that requires unearthing then exploring the assumptions that have brought about acceptance of many of the prevailing unfavorable attitudes about age. Only then can we determine whether those assumptions are valid, and, if they are, whether they will continue to pose problems in the new world of work.

Peeling the Onion

As our society has matured, we have come to recognize ever more forms of discrimination. Today, discrimination based on race, gender, or national origin instantly raises red flags. When it comes to age discrimination in the workplace, however, the zeal is far more muted, in part because the perceptions underlying the discrimination match so many of the perceptions and attitudes about age found in society in general. Even the terms used to describe older people in the media, such as "geezer," convey the discomfort many feel about aging. In part, this ambivalence occurs because the battles over age waged by senior citizens have revolved more around financial support in retirement than fairness in the workplace.

In the workplace, explaining the preference for younger workers has been elevated to an art, with care taken to avoid legal problems. The reasons, always carefully phrased when provided by management, range from lack of flexibility to younger managers' discomfort. When those who study corporations address the issue, the answers are far more revealing.

For example, John A. Challenger, an executive vice president of the outplacement firm Challenger, Gray & Christmas, Inc., says that the amount of severance and length of tenure of those being counseled indicates that "companies are targeting veteran workers for their layoffs and buyouts," replacing them with lower-cost juniors.[2] Peter Cappelli, the chairman of the University of Pennsylvania's Wharton Business School's Department of Management, says that some of the discrimination against displaced, older managers may be a result of the fear that "they're going to feel undercompensated and underused" and end up "making the people around them feel uncomfortable." Jerry Young, a former vice president of RCA Global Communications and cofounder of a now disbanded organization aimed at displaced executives, notes that "the stock reasons you hear are that older people are burnt out, that companies will have to fund your retirement, that you'll overload their medical insurance." He adds, "I don't think a 45-year-old CEO wants a father figure working under him."[3]

These statements are indicative of the attitudes that typically underlie discriminatory behavior, attitudes that have only a limited basis in reality. But even when there is a problem, solutions are usually easy to find. Moreover, many of the problems attributed to age often are found in other groups as well. For example, studies designed to uncover age discrimination show that when photos of workers were attached to comments about, say, learning new technologies, those evaluating the workers' willingness to learn always gave younger workers the benefit of the doubt on ambiguous statements. A younger worker's reluctance to begin a training program is excused because "he just left school and must be tired of sitting in a classroom all day." The older worker's desire to put off training until a later date is seen as resistance.

Since older workers are going to become an ever-larger percentage of the workforce, the realities behind the issue of age discrimination must be confronted. Edgar H. Schein, one of the pioneers of organizational development, has shown that unless the unexamined assumptions underlying the culture of an organization are brought to light, changing the culture is impossible.[4] Once people reach a greater understanding of what is behind their feelings about age, and not just age in the workplace, it will be far easier for everyone to come to terms with the subject of an aging workforce.

Have We Hung Up Our Gloves?

The 1960s brought about enormous social change in this nation. The era was marked by a strong economy and rebellious youth who had the time, education, and energy to fight for the abolition of all kinds of unfairness in order to improve life for all citizens. Minorities, malnourished children, and poverty-stricken seniors were among those targeted as in need of help. Civil rights laws, antipoverty programs, and improvements in Social Security were put in place. In 1967, the Age Discrimination in Employment Act was passed, prohibiting employment discrimination against persons forty years of age or older. The purpose of the act was "to promote employment of older persons based on their ability rather than age; to prohibit arbitrary age discrimination in employment; to help employers and workers find ways of meeting problems arising from the impact of age on employment."[5]

Few turned to the courts for redress in the years immediately following the act's passage, in part because many affected older workers found that the increases in Social Security payments and the attractions of retirement were preferable to long legal battles. The legislation began to attract more attention when the downsizings of the late 1980s began to take their toll most heavily on workers over fifty. The U.S. Equal Employment Opportunity Commission, which is responsible for enforcing the act by dealing with complaints about discrimination due to race, sex, disabilities, age, and national origin, found its workload increasing in the early 1990s. Downsized older workers, unable to find jobs at anything close to their old wages, took advantage of the act to file complaints against the companies that had let them go. In 1991, 17,550 charges were filed; over 19,000 a year were filed from 1992 to 1994. After that, although the displacement rates remained high, the numbers dropped to 17,416 in 1995, 15,719 in 1996, and 15,785 in 1997.[6]

Even though unemployment had begun to fall in those last three years, the jobs replacing those lost did not pay as well. Furthermore, the constant churning and repeated downsizings had worn people out. Individuals began to accept losing ground. Frustration with the process of adjudication and a number of court decisions favoring the argument that employment decisions based on salary were reasonable made filing complaints seem pointless.

For many workers, the corporate decision to hire younger, less-expensive workers was understandable. It fit with the decisions of those corporations to move to whatever city offered the biggest tax breaks, to build plants abroad to take advantage of lower-paid labor, and to hire part-time and contingent workers to save the cost of benefits. It also fit with a decline in society's interest in taking care of the less fortunate. The late 1990s proved a less gentle time for the have-nots; it was a world in which inequality in income and wealth increased, a growing number of people lacked health insurance, and women were forced to leave the welfare rolls for work but their child care needs were not addressed. All this was accepted with little protest. The boomers, those rebellious children of the 1960s who had helped bring about so many social programs, seemed to have lost their spirit.

It is unfair, however, to place all the blame for age discrimination on younger people. Robert Menchin, the author of *New Opportunities for Older Americans,* says that "discrimination is real in the sense that age bias does exist despite laws against it. But it is also unreal in the sense that a lot of older people just don't try to get a job. Age bias is in their own mind. They buy into the myth that employers don't need them or their skills."[7]

How Old Is Too Old?

The world is youth-oriented. Television advertisers target young and middle-aged viewers, and everyone strives to look and act young. This fascination with youth peaked as the baby boomers reached their teens and has remained fairly steady ever since. Although many who were part of the "Don't trust anyone over thirty" generation are now pushing fifty—and don't like it—there hasn't been a noticeable shift in general attitudes toward older people.

When it comes to the workplace, even managers who are themselves older boomers seem to share the belief that older is not wiser. In business, the term *up-and-coming* is reserved for those in their twenties and thirties. If someone hasn't made it to a fairly senior position by his mid-forties (in companies that still have hierarchies), he is unlikely to be given a job that would put him in line for a top spot in an organization. Then, as workers approach their late fifties, everyone assumes they'll be leaving soon, so they are given fewer opportunities and challenges. This, in turn, reduces the value of these workers as well as their confidence in their abilities and their worth. The expectation that older workers contribute less, are harder to retrain, and cost more for the value they provide has become a self-fulfilling prophecy.

Assumptions about age and performance are not uniform, however, depending to a great extent on the type of work involved. In the case of a judge or a college professor, occupations that involve decision making based on experience and learning, age is assumed to be a positive factor. When it comes to more creative fields, especially those involving an understanding of new trends and developments, such as advertising or programming, forty is often considered old. Given the larger market share that older citizens will soon represent when it comes to advertising, that may change. In the case of programming, part of the reason for hiring younger people is the speed with which these companies believe they need to get new programs to market to remain competitive.

The common view is not so much that someone older cannot do creative work but that older workers are often unwilling to work around the clock for weeks at a time to meet extraordinary deadlines. Somewhat older workers tend to have more competing responsibilities for their time, and they also have learned that their extra efforts will remain in organizational memory for a very short time. Thus, since creativity in the workplace so often involves developing new products or services and getting these innovative ideas quickly to market, success tends to come to those who have the time and will to expend all their energy on work.

Other categories of jobs where it is often thought that "younger is better" involve fast reflexes or an extraordinary amount of physical strength, such as policing and fire fighting. For most jobs that involve strength and dexterity, such as factory work, all that is necessary is to match tasks with the physical condition of workers. Although that means that a sixty-year-old in good shape and a thirty-year-old in poor shape could do the same job with equal results, that is not the usual case, and manufacturing work tends to pose problems for older workers.

Today, however, most Americans are engaged in information-related work where age should not matter. Still, as people grow older, they often react as though they will have the same feelings and work experiences in their fifties and sixties as their parents. They believe their careers are tapering off, and thus they put less effort into learning new things and actively involving themselves in such things as informal brainstorming sessions.

But such reactions are wrong. Workers must understand that the demands of work today are very different, as is the ability to meet them for most people. Desks have replaced assembly lines and the manipulation of information has replaced the manipulation of welding torches; these changes make a huge difference in the ability to continue to work at an older age. Moreover, those in their fifties and sixties are for the most part in far better physical condition than their counterparts a generation ago, and much that can go wrong with older bodies can now be repaired. Third, this group's financial situation is far different because lifestyles are less age-related than they once were, which makes financial need a part of the equation.

For example, many boomers started their families later than past generations did (first-time motherhood at forty is no longer unusual), and many men start second families even later. For these people, their fifties, sixties, and even seventies are more likely to mean paying for college tuition than saving something extra for retirement. Yesterday's grandparents may well be today's parents. In addition, the second group of boomers has not had the opportunities to accumulate wealth that the older members of their cohort did. They entered a job market that was clogged by older boomers and a housing market in which prices had been pushed up by the first of the boomers.

Assumptions and Realities

Even when assumptions are explored and recognized as incorrect, new realities take a long time to replace old attitudes. In addition, many of the assumptions may be rooted in past truths and remain applicable to some individuals. Genetics, lifestyles, and exposure to different environments make each time of life very different for each individual. In fact, according to recent research at the University of Minnesota, "there is even more heterogeneity within the older population than is true of other age groups."[8] Indeed, the fact that a few women in their late fifties and even early sixties have sustained a pregnancy does not mean that every woman that age could, even with the same medical care. Ninety-three-year-old marathoners are rare, and so are baseball players in their forties— but both exist.

To change the prevailing attitudes toward older workers, we must probe the assumptions that underlie them. The following are among the most damaging of the assumptions made.

Assumption: Perhaps the most strongly held assumption is that older workers are not as creative or productive as younger workers. Surveys reveal that senior management believes productivity begins to decline anywhere from fifty-one (Germany) to sixty-two (Singapore). Executives in the United States surveyed for

113

Competing in a Global Economy put the figure at sixty. An interesting side note is that worldwide, executives believe that productivity peaks, on average, at forty-three and holds fairly steady for about fifteen years after that.[9]

Reality: In manufacturing, older workers who had trouble keeping up tended to be pushed out of the workforce or to leave as early as possible. Today, the nature of manufacturing work has changed enough because of automation that some of those problems have been eliminated. In addition, there has been an enormous switch to knowledge work, where age plays little role in productivity.

When it comes to creative work, we have already noted that lack of time is more the issue than a lack of creativity. It also is noteworthy that those who work for large corporations usually encounter so many problems trying to get new ideas heard and approved that they stop trying after a while—again a self-fulfilling prophecy. The longer their ideas have been waffled over, ignored, or derided, the less likely they are to be interested in putting new ones forward. Experience also brings greater understanding about whether or not an idea will have market value. As a result, younger workers present a larger number of ideas but fewer that are valuable. When enthusiasm is tempered by reality, the results can be misleading. Measuring the number, source, and ultimate value of new ideas may be a useful exercise.

Assumption: Older workers are ill more often than younger workers.

Reality: Older workers tend to be absent from the workforce less often than younger workers. Although they do have more chronic conditions, those conditions usually do not incapacitate them. And although 13.6 percent of the workforce is over fifty-five, those over fifty-five account for only 9.7 percent of on-the-job injuries.[10] Workers over fifty file far fewer worker compensation claims; the largest number of claims are filed by those thirty to thirty-four. One explanation is that injuries tend to occur the first few weeks on the job. Another is that they are related to high-risk

114

occupations, which tend to attract fewer older workers. But there is evidence that experience has taught older workers to exercise more care and to ask advice and follow directions before acting.[11]

Assumption: Older workers are less flexible and adaptable than younger workers.

Reality: Although older workers are more likely to ask why a change is being made, it does not mean that they are unwilling to accept change. If companies thought about why these workers are asking such questions, they might begin to see their value. People who have worked for many years have seen many attempts to change processes and procedures that had to be abandoned midstream; older workers may know why these efforts did not bring results and see similarities in the new changes that lead them to think they will also fail. Companies hire consultants who have multiple experiences with a new process or technology because it is in their area of expertise and they have brought similar changes to many other companies. These companies are paying for the knowledge of what works and what doesn't in different kinds of companies. Since many older workers have similar accumulations of war stories, both from their experiences at other jobs with other organizations and from their years with their current employers, their hesitation to make a given change may be rooted in useful knowledge. Only if employees remain resistant after reasonable discussions and explanations can they be charged with inflexibility.

When they encounter what seems like resistance to a change, managers should look beyond individual cases and determine whether the resisters are all older and whether resistance continues or even increases with training. If it does, the training methods may be at fault.

Another reason to doubt this assumption is the number of workers who decide to switch careers in their late forties and fifties. Many of these workers take courses to augment their current skills; others pursue advanced degrees with an eye toward moving ahead; still others decide to enter a new field, sometimes with the goal of finding a new career path that will bring more personal satisfaction and allow them to work part-time after retirement.

Assumption: "You can't teach an old dog new tricks." In fact, "sixty-six percent of the respondents to a 1998 survey of human resources professionals agree that older workers tend to be more fearful of technology than younger workers."[12]

Reality: Curtis Plott, president of the American Society for Training and Development, says that boomers can learn new technologies as well as younger workers. However, he points out that "boomers are struggling like all the rest of us to keep up with the changing knowledge and skills we'll all need in the future."[13] Discussing the speed of technological change with technologists, especially young ones, makes the problem extremely clear. Statements such as "I was tied up on a project night and day for three months. When I came up for air and chatted with friends in the field, I discovered I'd fallen behind" are not uncommon.[14]

There is some truth to the charge that older workers fall behind in acquiring new skills. This is because they are not being given the same opportunities for training offered younger workers. A study by Craig Olson of the Industrial Relations Institute in Wisconsin shows that employees are given the most opportunities for training at the age of forty, the least after fifty-five.[15]

Those worried about older people's interest in and ability to learn new technology might be surprised to discover that the fastest-growing group of Internet users are those over fifty, according to a 1997 ACNielsen survey of North American Internet use. Today, many seniors use the Internet to look for travel bargains, learn about advanced medical treatments, and keep in touch with friends and family.

Assumption: Even if they can learn, it isn't worth retraining older workers because they do not stay on the job for very long.

Reality: Studies of tenure indicate that older workers are far less likely to leave a job than younger workers. The Bureau of Labor Statistics reported in 1998 that workers between forty-five and fifty-four had double the median years of tenure of those between twenty-five and thirty-four. According to the American Association of Retired Persons (AARP), workers between fifty and sixty stay on the job an average of fifteen years. The reality is that older workers stay with a company far longer because of the discrimination they know they will encounter when looking for new positions and because of their pensions. Since they learn as well as younger workers when training is tailored for them, their attendance is excellent, and their productivity is comparable, the basis for this assumption is invalid.

Furthermore, managers who accept this assumption often decide that older employees won't want to learn something new because they won't be on the job very long. That assumption may have been valid in the past, when full retirement was a norm, but many of today's older workers plan to remain involved in work post-retirement and are eager to ensure they have the skills to do so. And when technology training is provided for older workers, such as the program offered through an alliance of Microsoft Skills 2000, the Green Thumb, Inc., and the federal government, there has been no shortage of interested applicants.

Assumption: Older workers find it hard to take orders from younger workers, and younger workers don't like to give orders to people old enough to be their parents.

Reality: A survey by the Society for Human Resource Management (SHRM) and the AARP released in May 1998 found that only 21 percent of human resources managers surveyed agreed that younger managers tend to be uncomfortable supervising older workers, and 44 percent disagreed strongly. When it came to older worker discomfort when working with younger supervisors, the numbers were very similar, with 23 percent agreeing, and 44 percent disagreeing strongly.[16]

Another issue here is the leveling of hierarchies in the new world of work. Team work eliminates much of this problem and so does reporting online. At the same time, interactions between older and younger team members are complicated by issues of expectations, behavioral differences (manners, forms of address),

117

and lack of formal reporting mechanisms. Diversity training is a necessity in these situations.

Assumption: Older workers cost more than younger workers.

Reality: Workers with tenure are entitled to more vacation time, insurance companies charge companies that employ many older workers more, and pension costs are related to the number of years worked—even matching contribution plans cost more because older workers tend to contribute more. On the other hand, replacing workers is not cost-free. Replacements have to be recruited and trained, then they must adjust to the corporate culture, which adds to productivity costs. Aetna Insurance Company did a study of this problem in 1989 and discovered that these three factors alone cost 93 percent of first-year salary for new employees.[17]

Moving On

Fighting discrimination based on assumptions is not easy—it does not happen by itself. Uncovering one false or outdated assumption at a time and informing people of the new reality will not effect change. It takes a concerted effort to make people understand why they feel as they do—then to change the way they react to those feelings, if not the feelings themselves.

R. Roosevelt Thomas, the author of *Beyond Race and Gender* and a pioneer in developing plans for managing diversity, highlights the importance of involving the right people at the right level of the corporation as a first step. That step must then be followed by communicating the goals of the process, making sure that performance is recognized and rewarded, "providing career planning and training and development to help people grow, integrating work and family policies and programs to offer more flexible and appropriate benefits." Perhaps most important is putting programs in place and assigning accountability for their success.[18]

All this necessitates changing the managerial mindset about the value of older employees and teaching managers how to deal with an aging workforce. Highlighting the demographics should help make the need to change clear. However, it also is important to emphasize the value of older workers as sources of institutional memory and a means of spreading the corporate culture to new workers when they come on board. Presenting evidence of the ability of older people to be productive helps as well: Retirees working long hours for volunteer organizations, going back to school in record numbers, and spending time in athletic pursuits.

Another place to look for truths about the value and abilities of older workers is among those who solved the problem of being downsized by setting up their own businesses. Harry Schlegel, a successful salesman of technology equipment in the Pittsburgh area, decided on that course of action when an executive recruiter asked him, in the midst of a long, seemingly fruitless job search after the company he worked for went out of business: "Why don't you dye your hair?" Schlegel, who was fifty-one, had already been rejected numerous times when prospective employers figured out his age because of his service in Vietnam. Angry, he decided that he'd "had enough of other people controlling my future and decided I wanted to control it." He bought a cleaning company franchise and launched his company. When asked if his age and experience—barriers to reentering the workforce when he was seeking employment—were a problem as a business owner, he replied, "No, absolutely not. They were assets. I found that the skills I was offering to prospective employers were skills I could utilize myself to build a business." Harry Schlegel is not alone. Gray-haired business owners are treated with respect; they have succeeded in putting their years of experience to good use. Gray-haired prospective employees with exactly the same qualifications, however, are treated with skepticism bordering on disdain; they are seen as failures.[19]

As long as these attitudes prevail, retention programs will not be enough to keep people working past the point at which they believe they can retire comfortably. In addition to such programs, companies must develop measures to ensure that managers understand the value of older workers, manage them to the advantage of the organization, and integrate them into the culture rather than treating them as guests who have stayed too long at the party.

PART III

The Way Out

Chapter 6

Laying the Foundation

From the standpoint of the firm, employees are both potential assets which if mobilized and fully utilized can serve as a source of competitive advantage and costs that, if not controlled properly, will serve as a competitive liability. From the employee's perspective the firm provides both a job and the source of one's economic livelihood. . . . Alternatively, an employer can be a major source of economic insecurity, frustration, or stress in an employee's life.

Thomas Kochan[1]

Corporate America must take action now to survive the graying of the workforce. If corporations want to attract and retain committed, skilled workers in a future in which there will be too few workers, they will have to overcome the pervasive skepticism toward corporate intentions. Since this lack of trust in corporations is a result of the destruction of the old social contract, corporations will have to define a believable new social contract to replace the one they destroyed and convince workers that they will stand by it. That means the new contract must address the changes that have taken place in the world of work.

The first step must be to reduce workplace stress and anxiety to make it possible for employees even to hear what senior management has to say about a new social contract. The next step is to redefine the organization's mission. The third step is to define corporate goals that include strategies and actions to achieve the mission and to propose realistic time frames for reaching those goals.

The new social contract also must address three main issues: The way work is structured, training and retraining, and diversity. The purpose of the first is to retain workers as well as support the goal of so many older workers to work retired by building a workplace that accommodates and encourages flexibility while providing economic equity for those who opt for less than full-time work arrangements. The purpose of training and retraining, especially of older workers, is to ensure that they can continue to add value to the company. Diversity programs are necessary to ensure that all workers are treated fairly.

The new social contract is not a one-way street. It involves rights and obligations on both sides, and it requires, at times, the involvement of the public sector. Taken together, these broad strategies will pay off in the long term, when the only way to close the gap between the number of workers needed to maintain a constant total employment-to-population ratio will be, as noted earlier, to increase the labor force participation of those over fifty-five by about 25 percent.[2] For every older worker who decides not to extend his or her employment, corporations will have to convince younger workers to put in longer hours. Alternatively, they can focus on new ways to improve productivity and hope to find them in time to avert a crisis when the boomers reach retirement.

Larger corporations addressing this problem now face a number of challenges. For many, the strong economy, solid consumer demand, and happy shareholders make it hard to accept the need to change. Using contingent workers, providing as few benefits as possible, and replacing obsolete skills by replacing workers have kept profits high. Moreover, the workforce has not seized the moment offered by tight labor markets to push for higher salaries. Why, corporations ask, should they look for trouble? The answer is simple. Such short-term thinking has always had severe long-term costs. Being blinded by the rosy glow of success can be dangerous, a lesson IBM learned in the 1980s, when it ignored developments that soon eroded its client base. IBM remained wedded to mainframe computers long after client server technology utilizing personal computers became the choice of corporation after corporation.

Yet corporate leaders continue to bury their heads in the sand when it comes to the long term. Of course, these organizations also may be putting off acting now because they believe that when the time comes, they will only have to offer higher salaries than their competitors to become the workplace of choice. While fair salaries and decent benefits should be routine, bidding wars for workers can become dangerous, cutting profitability and producing inflation. It also is likely to fail to attract those anxious to escape the world of work—something few large organizations seem to understand.

A Taste of the Future

The tight labor markets that began as the twentieth century was drawing to a close received extensive coverage in the popular and business press. In part, such stories were attractive after years of bad news on the labor front. Another reason, though, was reporters' growing recognition of the demographics of the issue as a result of the constant focus on the problems the Social Security system was expected to face when the boomers retired. Still, the stories in the popular press might have served as more of a red flag to corporations if not for the fact that the labor shortages varied by location rather than being evenly spread across the nation. These shortages proved more of a problem in the heartland and in areas with larger populations of retirees than in the larger states where the headquarters of so many large organizations are located.

Those in corporate America who still do not recognize the severity of the problem might do well to remember that the states having the most problems with worker shortages are those with somewhat older average populations. Of course, in those states with older populations, because they have large populations of retirees, service-sector companies in local communities have found ways to deal with the lack of younger workers in their communities, and the solution, attracting older workers on a part-time basis, has worked well for them (see Box 6.1).

In some communities, however, the problem is somewhat different. For example, in 1999, Fargo, North Dakota, became the first metropolitan area in the nation to record an unemployment rate below 1 percent since 1990, when the Bureau of Labor Statistics began keeping such records. In an article about Fargo, *Newsweek* magazine proclaimed: "Creating workers is more urgent than creating jobs. . . . The infinitesimal jobless rate turned many bosses into supplicants for workers' favor."

The story went on to tell of the closing of a beef plant that employed two hundred and eighty-three people. Usually a loss of that many jobs would be a cause for great concern in a city Fargo's size, but Fargo officials were pleased because the plant had posed a number of environmental problems. Moreover, within days of the announced closing, a local turkey-processing plant ran ads offering jobs to those who had worked at the beef-processing plant. *Newsweek*'s comment: "You can't even stay fired in Fargo these days."[3]

Communities such as Columbus, Ohio, and Omaha, Nebraska, awoke to the fact that the labor shortages they were experiencing were tremors announcing the quakes that the aging of the boomers would bring. These cities are having trouble attracting new businesses. Companies initially interested in relocating discover, when they investigate the available labor pool, that there aren't enough

Box 6.1
McDonald's Corp.

McDonald's has a long history of employing seniors. Barry Mehrman, director at the Human Resources Design Center at McDonald's Oak Brook, Illinois, headquarters, highlighted the success of the company's efforts to attract and retain older workers. He noted that in the 1980s, McDonald's established a six-week McMasters program for older recruits, an offshoot of their effort to recruit those with disabilities; the program has been "discontinued because we discovered that older workers did not need special training. The normal training program for all workers was enough."

When it comes to employee tenure, Mehrman says that seniors have the best record of all employees. He mentioned one former employee, an investment banker who came to McDonald's after retiring in his fifties. He began as a part-time worker, became an hourly manager, then was promoted to help in McDonald's senior recruitment efforts, doing community outreach. "This second career lasted long enough," Mehrman noted, "for him to earn the eight-week sabbatical McDonald's provides managers who have been with the company for at least ten years." He also mentioned a ninety-four-year-old worker in Chicago who had been with the company for eighteen years.

Mehrman said that recruitment was done through developing relationships in the community, so that McDonald's recruiters are welcomed, for example, at centers where possible workers might congregate, young or old. Seniors take these jobs because they offer flexible hours, a chance to get out of the house, and interaction with a diverse workforce. "Sixteen- and sixty-year-olds work side-by-side," Mehrman noted, which provides opportunities for building bridges between the generations.

When it comes to benefits, anyone working in a company-owned restaurant a thousand hours a year is eligible to participate in their 401(k) plan. Other benefits depend on the individual McDonald's. Mehrman also noted that in some areas, especially those with higher numbers of retirees, such as Florida, older worker participation was higher than in others, but he estimated that older workers were about 7 percent of the overall workforce.

Mehrman said that the employment of older workers was a "long-term strategy that the company hoped would serve them well in the future."

Source: Author interview.

prospective employees, much less skilled ones. These communities are attacking the problem through programs to improve the skills of the small number of unskilled and undereducated unemployed or to keep their young people from leaving after college by providing financial aid in return for promises to remain in the community for a specified time. While both kinds of programs may help, and improving the employability of those the system has failed is invaluable to our society, they will not provide an answer to a national, even an international, problem—the coming worker shortfall.

Developing Strategies for Winning Workers

Before formulating solutions to the coming turmoil, it is important to review the decisions that caused the problem. A major reason older people retire from work early and younger people dislike large organizations is the downsizings that changed the model of work. It is not the *fact* of the downsizings—most people have come to understand why companies had to change—but the way they were handled that has left such a residue of bad feelings. No one directly affected or even those who watched from the sidelines is likely to forget the following:

- *Companies weren't honest about what they were planning.* They often denied that downsizings were going to happen until they announced them, then escorted those affected out the door to buses that took them to outplacement centers.
- *Many downsizings were applied across the board.* In company after company, the same percentage of every department was downsized, when targeting departments by workload would have made far more sense and left far fewer workers having to do the work of those let go.
- *Companies took a revolving-door approach.* New hires were brought in to replace workers who might have been re-trained.
- *Many workers lost their middle-class lifestyle.* At the same time, top leadership and shareholders kept getting richer.
- *The workforce became so lean that people found themselves working longer and harder with few rewards.* Retained workers knew they faced a constant threat of being the next ones down-sized no matter how hard they worked.
- *Older workers were disproportionately affected by downsizing.*

The second cause of the coming problem involves the current retirement norm. People have to be encouraged to find alternatives to the ideal of retirement that developed in the 1960s and 1970s. Companies must develop and implement plans that do not automatically assume complete retirement, then encourage older workers to consider these alternatives when making their retirement decisions.

The third cause is discrimination—various forms of ageism in companies, among both managers and older workers who accept the all too common assumption that older employees provide less value. The result is a failure to offer training to older workers or to think of older workers as contributors to the bottom line.

Moving Forward

The next step is to address these issues directly in an attempt to keep older workers in the workplace longer or to bring some of them back into corporate America.[4] The broad efforts needed are as follows:

- Address the causes of worker stress and anxiety.
- Put in place corporate communications programs to provide realistic and useful information.
- Develop a mission statement accompanied by concrete strategies that, if enacted, will help corporations rebuild their reputations as ethical and trustworthy organizations.

In addition, companies can put in place numerous specific programs to retain older workers and make themselves more attractive to younger ones:

- Flexible work structures
- Training and retraining programs
- Diversity programs
- Portable benefits.

Since programs such as these take time to make a difference, and companies will not be able to do all of these things on their own, the time to begin is now.

New Beginnings

Before outlining specific recommendations for change, it is useful to examine examples of what works. Unfortunately, when one looks to corporations for such models, the results are disappointing. Call after call to human resource departments brings the same response: "No, I don't know of a specific program in place to deal with retention . . . with retraining older workers. We're doing something with a community program to improve the skills taught at the schools in our area. Oh, yes, someone in one of our departments has called back a few older workers. . . . Perhaps you should call someone at Company X or Y . . . they might be doing something."

Until 1999, the places that you were told to call because they offered such programs were always the same—a handful of primarily service companies that had developed such programs for older workers years ago because they were having trouble finding employees who would stay with them for more than a few months (see Box 6.2). Now, however, the tight labor markets have added new companies to the list. These companies tend to be either service-sector firms that need many low-wage workers or organizations that need highly skilled workers with a deep understanding of technology.

Companies such as Marriott and Burger King have a hard time keeping workers in a strong economy because as soon as the low-skilled, entry-level workers they hire gain experience, they can find work elsewhere. As a result, these companies have set up training programs for new employees, many of whom were on welfare, that teach very basic skills, including literacy and sometimes even life skills, such as how to manage a checking account.[5] At the same time, large consulting firms such as Pricewaterhouse-Coopers and Ernst & Young have developed elaborate retention programs to keep their consultants from leaving in response to offers from competitors or clients, as companies scramble to recruit people with hard-to-find skills.

While surveying companies to discover examples of successful

131

Box 6.2
Days Inns of America

In 1986, Days Inns of America actively began looking for workers over the age of fifty to work as reservation agents. The company was having major problems maintaining a steady workforce in Atlanta and Knoxville, the cities in which its sophisticated twenty-four-hour-a-day telecommunications centers for handling reservations were located. With annual turnover approaching 100 percent, the company was desperate for a solution to its staffing problem.

Days Inns of America, one of the largest hotel chains in the nation, is a franchise operation bound by a national toll-free reservation system. The job of reservation agent is complex but not unlike many jobs involving computerized operations today. Airline reservation agents, home shopping services (catalog, television, online), and insurance customer service agents perform the same functions. "Each agent must simultaneously engage in conversation with the prospective client, query the reservations system for information, report on data appearing on the [computer screen], while obtaining local amenity and environmental information for clients," according to William McNaught and Michael Barth, who have studied those systems.

The Days Inns executives who decided to hire older people to work with new technology that required multitasking and speed knew they were going against conventional wisdom. On the other hand, the work was sedentary and did not demand a great deal of physical dexterity, which, they felt, mitigated that risk.

At first, the recruiting efforts met with little success; few people responded to the advertisements placed in local papers, probably because most assumed the company had mentioned "all ages" merely to satisfy equal employment opportunity requirements. Management found that active recruitment efforts were necessary at such places as senior citizen centers, but over time word of mouth continued to bring in applicants.

In the beginning, it seemed as though training was going to pose a problem; older workers took a few days longer than younger ones to grow accustomed to the computer equipment. That problem was solved by adding a half-day of computer familiarization for older workers, after which younger and older workers were trained for the same amount of time. An in-depth study revealed that other anticipated difficulties also turned out to be exaggerated. For example, health costs were the same for older and younger workers (older people who choose to work tend to be healthier than those who do not, and older workers are less likely to have dependents that need coverage).

Concerns about productivity due to the increased length of each call made by older workers proved groundless when those calls resulted in more bookings. The most important advantage of hiring older workers was the sharp improvement in retention rates—three years instead of one. The result was less need for training for new hires, which more than made up for an extra half-day spent on computer familiarization.

Source: William McNaught and Michael C. Barth, "Are Older Workers 'Good Buys'?" *Sloan Management Review* 33, no. 3, March 1992, pp. 53 ff.; Commonwealth Fund, *The Untapped Resource* (New York: Commonwealth Fund, 1993), p. 17; various stories in the business press.

programs, some experts offered extremely helpful general insights. For example, Donna Martin, a senior human relations executive for almost two decades with Bell Atlantic Corporation, Baxter Health Care, Inc., and Monsanto, who is currently head of human resources for Global Pharmaceutical Operations North America for Pharmacia & Upjohn, supports the finding that little has been done to date.[6]

Martin says that companies are not yet "paying a lot of attention to the problem of retention. There are even forward-looking companies that are not fully aware of what they are going to be facing, which is somewhat frightening." One reason for this, she says, may be that human resources departments "are still focused on the problems of recruiting new 'young' talent and helping workers who may be pushed out or choose to be more mobile workers. As a result, they are focusing on such things as making pension plans portable, which gives people the ability to move around more easily." She added that "many of these efforts to ensure that workers who aren't needed long-term have protection will work in favor of the companies providing them, if they need to hire many people for short periods of time in the future, especially in the area of technology where people switch jobs frequently."

Martin's comments are far more enlightened than most. The blindness in many quarters is somewhat startling: According to a 1995 survey of Fortune 200 human resources directors by the Human Resources Institute, by 2005 the fourth-highest concern for human resources departments will be an aging workforce.[7] That means that a mere six years before the first of the baby boomers are old enough to retire at full benefits—let alone retire early— companies finally will begin to address the issue.

HR Magazine projects that "the squeeze in labor will push HR more prominently into the executive suites of corporate America. The front office will rely more heavily on HR for strategic business decisions based on the type of skills available in the market."[8] The issue, however, is far broader than making decisions based on "the type of skills available in the market." Companies will not be able to find the workers they need if they don't act now to become employers of choice—that is, if they don't begin to develop policies that will gain them a reputation as good places to work when the choice is that of workers.

Stress Reduction

In late 1998, I was asked to participate in a series to be broadcast on National Public Radio. The subject, which eventually became the title of the five-part series, was "Anger in the Workplace." All the participants were asked by R. Brayton Bowen of the Howland Group, who was the host of the series, to be prepared to discuss the underlying causes of the anger so prevalent among American workers. During the discussions, all the participants agreed that workplace anger was a result of high stress levels resulting from uncertainty about their jobs, the pressure to do more work for the same rewards, a lack of understanding of what was expected, and a lack of communication not only about their roles and responsibilities but about their companies' plans and progress.

How Bad Is It?

According to a survey of 1,800 workers by Aon Consulting in 1998, the percentage of workers reporting "stress to the point of burnout" rose from 39 percent in 1995 to 53 percent in 1998, while personal life stress remained about the same—27 percent in 1995 and 28 percent in 1998. One effect of this increased stress at work is a decrease in productivity. The same survey reports that the "average time missed for stress has increased 36 percent since 1995."[9] *Business Week* noted in 1998 that "illness, long the chief cause of work absences, has lost ground to newer excuses: 'stress' and 'entitlement mentality'—i.e., 'I've worked my tail off; I deserve time off.' "[10]

The effects of stress are apparent at every level. Exec-U-Net, a job search company in Norwalk, Connecticut, found that "34 percent of unemployed executives were willing to take a pay cut if their new jobs would have less stress. And nearly half of fifty-one to fifty-five-year-old executives wanted to simplify their lives in order to spend more time with friends and family."[11]

The Families and Work Institute of New York reports that employees feel they are being pushed too hard. Indeed, of 2,877 employees they surveyed in 1998, 88 percent said they had been working "very hard," 68 percent reported they had been working "very fast," 60 percent said that they never had enough time to do their work, and 18 percent said that they "have to work overtime with little or no notice at least once a week."[12] Although the reality may be somewhat less daunting than these perceptions, these people's feelings will determine their future actions.

What Causes It?

Stress has multiple causes, ranging from the extra work that comes with lean organizations to the need to keep adapting to new technologies and new corporate structures to the uncertainties that are now a part of the new world of work. For example, 23 percent of employees in the Aon 1998 survey reported working more than fifty hours a week on average, a jump of 10 percent since 1995.[13] Other studies report that the amount of extra work is far lower. Some argue that workers stay at work long hours because they prefer it to what they face at home, especially in families where both parents work and the home front is chaotic. Still others say workers put in extra time because they believe that "face time" convinces their bosses that they are working hard for the company, which may make a difference in a future downsizing or when a scarce opportunity for promotion arises.

Stress is also created by the information overload caused by advanced communications and information technology. The amount of information that people must process today can be overwhelming. A survey by Pitney Bowes, Inc., of Stamford, Connecticut, reports that the average worker in an administrative to senior executive position in a large organization today receives about 190 messages daily. Reading and listening to so many e-mails, phone calls, and faxes and deciding what to respond to and when can take up to several hours a day. Respondents reported that their "feelings of being overwhelmed by the demands of communication correlate directly with having to constantly reprioritize work and juggle schedules to keep up with the volume of messaging."[14]

Technology also increases stress because it has made work inescapable. Pagers, beepers, cell phones, faxes, and laptops all tie people to work during vacations, ball games, even dinner parties and concerts. People answer calls in their cars, fax documents from airports, and receive and send e-mails in the middle of the night. When the telephone was introduced, one of the marketing claims was that it allowed the owner of a business to go on vacation and keep in touch with his company. Today, it seems as though everyone at every level is connected—all the time.

Solutions

A "stress-free" work environment is probably an oxymoron, but a less stressful one is not. There are many ways to reduce workplace stress, ranging from teaching time-management techniques and methods of prioritization to providing clear job descriptions and putting feedback mechanisms in place.

Time Management

In a world of lean organizations, overabundant information, and jobs that have few boundaries, a day's work can be endless. E-mails, phone calls, and meetings eat up enormous amounts of time. E-mail is particularly troublesome because it is easy to send multiple copies to a long list of people with one click.

The following would help improve the abilities of employees to manage their time:

- *Develop online scheduling capability.* One way to help employees better manage their time is to make online calendars a part of normal operations. These calendars contain information about deadlines and meetings. For example, a team member who wanted to schedule Bob and Sue for a meeting could check each of their calendars online, find a time they are both free—noting that Tuesday wouldn't be good because Sue is scheduled to give a major presentation later that day—and enter the chosen date on his own and Bob's and Sue's schedules with a request for confirmation. The rounds of calls and callbacks that usually are needed to schedule such meetings could therefore be reduced or avoided.

- *Control the amount of unnecessary information that is circulating.* In a world in which there is an overabundance of information, everyone must be made aware of the problem and trained to make reasonable judgment calls. Who really needs to know what? Labeling documents to make clear what needs attention now and what can wait—and what is merely a courtesy copy rather than a critical message—is one such step. How many times does your computer interrupt you with a notice that "you have mail" when you are expecting an important piece of information, then when you interrupt your work to open the mail, the message is a plea for a home for a stray cat someone has found? Companies must address this kind of disruption not only to prevent stress but to eliminate unproductive distractions.

  Teaching people how to use the Internet to prepare materials for presentation or do research effectively is a great help. Providing access to paid services such as Lexis or Northern Light, which can provide far more targeted information than general searches, is also helpful. Such services tend not only to save time, but because employees have to make fewer decisions about the relative usefulness of the material, they also reduce employee stress.

- *Schedule uninterrupted work time.* Companies can allow individuals to schedule—and post—times when they will be unavailable. Two hours a day of uninterrupted time can increase overall productivity—and creativity—enormously. The time for "uninterrupted work" is easiest to schedule in companies with flextime arrangements. If employees can choose to work their eight hours from eight to four, nine to five, or ten to six, the two uninterrupted hours can be before or after the "common" work day.
- *Make sure meetings are effective and efficient.* Meetings must begin and end on time, agendas must be set and adhered to, and issues that cannot be resolved without additional input must be tabled and addressed at a later date. Workers who waste time pontificating, arguing, and raising inappropriate subjects need to be trained in meeting behavior.
- *Encourage employees to keep personal logs.* By keeping track of their time, workers can pinpoint what causes them the most difficulty in time management. Group meetings then can be held to discuss and resolve time problems.

PRIORITIZATION

When employees constantly have more work than they can do, it can cause mental paralysis. Multitasking has become a norm, but there is an enormous difference between the ability to handle various aspects of a number of projects at the same time and being responsible for completing too many large tasks under impossible deadlines.

The leanness of organizations poses additional problems. If a member of a department is ill, who can be assigned to fill in? Today, secretaries and assistants work for many rather than just one or two individuals, which means they are not able to pick up the slack when someone is out. In the past, an assistant eventually learned enough about the position of the boss to be able to do a great deal of that work if the boss was unavailable. (Moreover, the one-on-one relationship provided mentoring and prepared a worker for internal promotion. As a result, such employees developed a great deal of loyalty to the organization.) In addition, in today's environment, temporary help is an option only if a worker is out for an extended period. If the absence is brief, his or her work must be done by the other members of the department. That would not be a major problem if those fellow employees knew that some assignments could be put aside. In flattened organizations, however, especially those that use many teams, that is not always the case because it is often unclear which goals take precedence, even to managers. To remedy this situation, companies should make a concerted effort to do the following:

- *Prioritize projects.* Management must learn to articulate corporate priorities in keeping with broader corporate goals. Employees at all levels must be kept abreast of the goals that are considered the highest priority so that they can decide when to question those in authority about conflicting priorities.
- *Establish an ombudsman or negotiator position to deal with conflicts.* Nothing creates more stress for employees than the feeling that they cannot win because they cannot decide what they should focus on. An official counsel to whom they could turn to settle conflicting demands would greatly reduce stress, especially if anonymity were ensured.

JOB DESCRIPTIONS

The organizational flattening and teamwork that is now a corporate norm often creates confusion about an individual's responsibilities and to whom he or she reports—that is, who is responsible for performance reviews. Organizations can do a number of things to eliminate such confusion:

- *Give every employee a clear job description.* Outlining responsibilities, authority, and reporting relationships makes employees feel more comfortable with their jobs. In companies where workers report to several managers, each manager needs to know how many hours of a given employee's time he or she is entitled to and who else has claims on that employee's time. Employees also need to know how to allocate their time among assignments.
- *Review job descriptions periodically.* The nature of work and the skill sets needed to do it change frequently in today's flexible organizations. If a new skill is needed, the employee should be allowed to take training sessions without constant interruptions to work on projects for other supervisors. As job descriptions change, rewards have to be adjusted to meet the new descriptions.

FEEDBACK

Employees who work on projects, especially those who prepare reports and recommendations, but never receive comments about their work do not continue to achieve at the same level. If they are not clear about the value of their work, they may decide there are problems with the way they did the work. As a result of performance anxiety, they may waste time trying a new approach when what they were doing was fine. On the other hand, if an employee's work is not providing value, no improvement will occur if no one explains what is wrong and how to change.

- *Respond rapidly.* Every time employees are asked to do something they have never done before, they must be told as soon as possible whether they are meeting expectations, and if they are not, they must be helped to find a better way to do the assignment. Work that is done repeatedly must be evaluated frequently to note if it is deviating from the standards, and excellence must be noted as well.

- *Provide frequent feedback.* Annual performance reviews are not enough to maintain morale. Rewards such as thank-you notes, public commendations, and office celebrations can augment formal reviews and maintain morale, particularly in stressful situations.
- *Establish appropriate training programs.* When an aspect of a job or the skills needed to accomplish it change and training is needed, choose workers with better-than-average skills and track records for learning to be the first trained. Their reports on the training program will set a tone that will reduce the anxiety of those who are not as comfortable with learning. The temptation to send the weakest employees first so that they will have more time to practice can backfire if they become negative and discouraged. Those who are likely to have problems also should be trained later because then they can get help from those who already have mastered the new skills.

Communication: Getting the Word Out

While these techniques help reduce stress, they will not eliminate it because change, which is a major cause of workplace stress, has become a constant. Mergers and acquisitions are always being announced, along with projections of layoffs; companies decide to outsource the work of whole departments; new products that require new skills come into demand; new competitors appear seemingly overnight. The knowledge that those changes might occur at any minute, eliminating jobs—even job categories—also creates stress. Employees worry that they will be blindsided by changes, not only within their company but in their industrial sector and even in the world of work. Good information about external developments as well as about changes within the organization can help alleviate those fears.

Although keeping current may be the responsibility of the individual, the reality is that most employees need help. Since employees constantly feel they need to look over their shoulders to find out what new developments in the business world might affect them, they worry about how to track those developments. They know they ought to be reading more to collect information about new processes and information and communications technologies. For example, they know they need to find out what their company is doing about E-business, and they wonder whether there is another concept such as downsizing being promoted by "experts" that might affect them. The list of concerns is endless, making it difficult to know where to start.

Corporate communications channels can help reduce the stress involved in trying to keep up with change. Some organizations put a great deal of effort into providing their employees (and their clients) with publications that serve as useful educational tools. One example is Hewlett-Packard, one of the world's largest computer companies, a source for everything from palmtops to printers and supercomputers, and a leading producer of test and measurement instruments. Headquartered in Palo Alto, California, Hewlett-Packard employs 120,000 people around the world, making it one of the top twenty companies on the Fortune 500 list. It is fifth among *Fortune*'s Most Admired Companies and tenth among *Fortune*'s Best Companies to Work for in America.

Besides its research and training centers, Hewlett-Packard reaches out through communications vehicles to ensure its employees and clients are up-to-date not only on what the company is doing but on developments and trends in technology and business. It conveys this kind of educational, in-depth information primarily through two flagship publications. The first is *Perspectives,* a quarterly newsletter featuring stories about what other companies are doing, general developments in business, reviews of business books, and explanations of important developments by different groups and divisions in the company. The other publication is the *IT Journal*, a somewhat more technical publication, presenting articles by experts in various fields, with comments by other experts.

Since not all companies can afford the Hewlett-Packard approach, they can establish other measures to help employees keep informed. For example, some companies set up article exchanges, provide a library, or see to it that important journals, both general and trade, are made easily available to interested employees.

Communicating with employees about internal developments is even more critical, given the universal fear of change. (Machiavelli's words about those who bring change remain true today: "The initiator has the enmity of all who would profit by the preservation of the institutions and merely lukewarm defenders in those who would gain by the new one."[15]) The more information employees have about coming changes, the more time they will have to adjust to them, and the less they will be disturbed by them.

Frequent communications with employees also help stop rumors, thus preventing the spread of misinformation and disinformation. Moreover, companies can use communications channels to present information on changes taking place elsewhere that, employees then realize, could be harmful to the company's position. This lays the groundwork for acceptance of the necessity of making similar changes.

Leaders must take a very visible role in the communications effort. Reports, letters, and memos from those in charge of the organization can be used to reassure, reward, and reconcile far more effectively than the same message coming from human resources or corporate communications departments. The personal message from the leader is a critical component when it comes to the next aspect of building a "choice" workplace—creating a reputation for trust, honesty, and ethics.

Retouching the Picture

Companies with a reputation for not caring for their employees will have a particularly hard time creating a culture that attracts workers, but it can be done. First, such companies must put in place and make public a statement of their ethics and values as part of a realistic mission statement, and take a series of actions to prove their commitment to it. Such firms must avoid making statements that they will regret—and not be able to live up to—the minute the economy falters or a new competitor emerges: Promising less, and delivering, is the key to rebuilding their reputations.

Since there will be times when living up to the contract will affect the company's bottom line, approval from the corporate board is a necessity. For example, everyone must accept that there will be times when the market's reactions to expenditures made to live up to their promises will create problems, but leaders committed to enforcing the contract and sure of their board's support can face down agitated stockholders if the commitment is of limited scale and duration. A promise of ensuring future employability, which would require providing extra training to employees being downsized, may mean that the company will not gain as much from an announced downsizing, but that promise will be easier to keep than the old promises of lifetime employment and should be doable.

People also have lost faith in the intentions of most corporations when it comes to the values and ethics proclaimed in their credos and mission statements. A few exceptions, such as Johnson & Johnson, have made such beliefs a centerpiece of their culture. The actions of Johnson & Johnson during one incident—the malicious tampering with its over-the-counter medication Tylenol—is considered the corporate gold standard. The company issued an instant recall, spread the information to the public, and handled the crisis with total grace. When one discusses the company with its employees, no matter what personal complaints they may have against it, there is a sense of pride in working for a company that has such a good reputation for honesty and caring.

It is time for many organizations to rethink and revise their mission statements. If an organization has a negative reputation as a result of its actions toward workers in the 1990s, it should revise the message to spell out what it intends to do for employees in the future. That is hard to do in the mission statement itself, which is a public document. For internal consumption, however, some organizations are beginning to augment these public statements with statements that detail how the mission will be carried out.

These strategic plans should set forth the company's goals and the programs it will initiate to achieve them.[16] For example, if a company's statement of its mission or objectives says, as Texaco's does, that its responsibilities toward its employees include "recogniz[ing] the dignity of the individual by treating every person in the company with respect and courtesy," the company should have strategies to ensure this is done. Diversity training programs and a process for reporting violations should be available to support the objective set forth in the statement. Texaco's recent embarrassment over its alleged treatment of African-American employees, which ended up in a messy court case, made its mission statement seem a farce. As a response to the publicity, the company finally established a comprehensive diversity program clearly supported by senior management.

Ideally, the mission statement should be prominently displayed and referred to frequently so that the message will be clear that management takes it seriously and will try to live up to it. In addition, the strategies for ensuring that the mission is carried out also must be widely available so employees accept the company's commitment to them. By including a time frame for action on new initiatives, such as adding training programs or appointing an ombudsman to handle complaints about discrimination, the company gives employees a way to hold them accountable if they fail to act, thus ensuring action as a means of self-protection. While the mission statement should not be revisited yearly, the statements of action should be reviewed at predetermined—and preannounced— times. Progress reports should be made and the addition of new programs and changes in or the elimination of old ones should be announced. This is not an easy road to take, but openness is going to be a critical success factor in rebuilding the social contract.

Donna Martin, the head of human resources for Global Pharmaceutical Operations North America for Pharmacia & Upjohn, says that what "strikes me most is walking the talk; it is being truthful and honest and respectful with people in the relationship you have with them as a corporation, and it is establishing a set of values around which you are going to operate and that you live by.

"You don't always have to like what you are being told in an organization. There are some things that are not totally controllable. Conditions change. People understand that, but what they want, I've discovered through the counselling I do, is that the company be honest and respect people as intelligent human beings who will contribute if given the opportunity."

No End in Sight

Reducing stress through such clarifications of expectations and open communication is necessary for companies that want to ensure their future success. At the same time, it is important to remember that this is only the tip of a very large iceberg. Martin says that when she was a vice president for human resources at Baxter Health Care, she set up a task force to look at the issue of how the company could attract workers in a competitive environment even though people with necessary skills were scarce. In doing this, she says, they determined that "you go about establishing mutual respect with your workers; you provide for them the goods and services that will make it comfortable for them to work; you pay competitively, you don't have to be off the scale, but you pay reasonably and fairly for what it is you are asking them to do; you provide them with the level of flexibility they may need; you provide any other kinds of assistance that might be needed such as elder care and child care."

Each of the points she mentions will take a company in the direction of a new social contract, but other things also need to be done. The broken promises about lifetime employment in good jobs that once made possible the American dream of home ownership and a proper pension have made skepticism and cynicism about corporate intentions the new norm. Full-time employees working side by side with former employees who are now contingent and temporary help see themselves in a similar position and shudder. Every announcement about adopting new software, new systems, new processes is a threat. How close is that abrupt termination, which is likely to be followed by employment at less pay and with less prestige? Promises of retraining, adequate notice, and fair pay for growth are worthwhile only if employees believe them. Companies must remember that every violation of the new arrangements they put in place will further damage their image, making it ever harder to survive the worker shortfall of the coming decades.

Chapter 7

Building the Framework

To maintain our dynamic economy and to fill the jobs of the 21st century, we must make the most of the creative potential and productive capacity of this growing segment of our society.

President Bill Clinton, Proclamation declaring National Older Workers Employment Week (1998)

The next step in developing the new social contract is establishing three kinds of specific programs. The first program will structure the way jobs are defined to ensure more flexibility for workers. The second will provide training and retraining. The third will ensure that workers who do not fit the majority profile are accepted and treated fairly and that their specific needs are accommodated. Although the aim of this book is to ensure that corporations address the aging of the workforce and the coming need to recruit and retain older workers, most of the goals of these programs will be equally attractive to younger workers.

Workers close to or past retirement age want flexible jobs so they will have time to do the things they have always put off because of work. Younger workers want flexible work because they want time to devote to family and personal growth.

149

When it comes to training, all workers, regardless of age, have to renew their skills continuously because of the speed of technological innovation. It has been widely noted that a career lasts about four-and-a-half years today; in other words, half of the knowledge and skills needed to do a job, which are honed in the first couple of years on the job, will be obsolete about two years later. Those who work in the area of technology face an even more difficult learning curve; for example, software engineers can find their current skills obsolete in less than a year.

All workers want opportunities to participate in training, and they all want a chance to be part of the organization. Moreover, the ethnic shifts that are about to occur in the composition of the workforce make elimination of discrimination even more important. Demographic projections indicate not only that there will be more older workers but that, for example, the Hispanic population will increase from 11.4 percent in 2000 to 18.9 percent in 2030, and the Asian population will increase from 4.1 percent in 1990 to 7 percent in 2030.

Taking Action

Some organizations have already begun to address the needs of older workers. A 1998 survey of 2,717 human resources managers by the Society for Human Resource Management and the AARP found the following:

- 62 percent said they hire retired employees as consultants
- 47 percent provide training to upgrade older-worker skills
- 29 percent provide opportunities for workers to transfer to jobs with reduced pay and responsibilities
- 19 percent have a phased retirement program that gradually reduces work schedules
- 10 percent provide alternative career tracks for older workers.[1]

More effort is clearly needed. Responsibility for developing these programs and ensuring that they appeal to younger as well as older workers must be given to the right departments and the right people. Of course, without leadership support, none of this will succeed. George Bailey, Watson Wyatt's global director of human capital, makes very clear the need for support from the top. He says that "companies are telling us that innovation and creativity are ever more crucial for building competitive advantage. What they need to do is devote the same board-level attention to human capital management as they have to all other organizational assets."[2]

The largest burden, however, is going to fall on those working in human resources and training. *HR Magazine* says that "HR experts foresee the need for fundamental changes in recruitment, training, and retention efforts. Employers will need strategies to help them spot new skills, hire quickly, retrain staff and keep the firm competitive amid constant turbulence in the labor force." But according to David Peterson, senior vice president of Personnel Decisions International of Minneapolis, "Right now we're just scratching the surface on what this is going to look like in a few years. . . . We'll need a whole new infrastructure."[3]

New Models of Work

The definition of *job* is no longer limited to full-time, permanent, salaried work. Over the past decade, alternative models have developed, and most companies offer a mix of employment arrangements, ranging from full-time, permanent work on-site to part-time, temporary telecommuting. The impetus behind many of these new arrangements has been the need to augment the lean full-time staffs most organizations maintain today. The motive for leanness is more than cost, although in the current competitive environment that remains an important issue. Companies also turn to these less-permanent arrangements because of a reluctance to fall into the trap of expanding the workforce only to reduce it later. They are aware of the financial and psychological costs that such actions entail.

As a result, when there is a sudden increase in work today, a project that needs to be done more quickly than usual, or someone who can't keep up, alternate arrangements are made. The typical organization now has numerous categories of workers, and more are likely to be developed as the workplace continues to evolve.

Full-time Permanent Work

Although full-time permanent work is still the norm, according to the Bureau of Labor Statistics more than 25 percent of the full-time workforce had made flexible scheduling arrangements in 1997—more than double the number in 1991. The higher the position, the higher the percentage with flexible arrangements. The most common flexible arrangements for full-time workers are flextime (people start their day at a time of their choosing between 8:00 A.M. and 10:00 A.M. and leave eight hours later) or compression (these arrangements tend to involve either working nine days in two weeks or four ten-hour days a week).

Part-time Permanent Work

These jobs are for fewer than forty hours a week. They may call for two or three full-time days, five half-time days, or any other combination, but they are not limited in duration. Included in this category is the somewhat new concept of shared jobs, a development promoted by new mothers who wanted to reduce their time at work for a few years but not leave the workforce completely. Some companies are good about providing prorated benefits for those who work under these arrangements, and Internal Revenue Service regulations address the problem of companies that label workers "independent contractors" when they work more than a certain number of hours a week. These regulations help ensure that these workers receive the same benefits that full-time workers do. (See below for a discussion of job sharing as a preretirement strategy.)

Full-time and Part-time Temporary Work

This category encompasses a number of job arrangements. Contingent work, usually defined as work not expected to last, accounts for about 5 percent of the workforce. Although most of these jobs are in the service sector, particularly sales, about 20 percent of these workers are ranked as professional. The majority of individuals in these jobs are under thirty-five.

As Table 7.1 shows, in the years since the push toward a more flexible organizational structure began, there has been an increase in the number of workers hired through companies that provide temporary help. Today, one of those companies, Manpower, Inc., is the nation's largest employer. Finding workers became the biggest problem facing these organizations as labor markets tightened in the late 1990s, and they have, as a result, targeted older workers.

A significant development in this area is the use of former employees, often retirees, who return to the organizations from which they have retired on a temporary basis. Travelers Corporation, a pioneer in this area, set up such a service for retired workers some two decades ago and has had such success with it that other companies have adopted similar programs (see Box 7.1). This approach is extremely beneficial because former workers understand the organization's culture and how it works.

Contract or Consulting

There are few standards for these arrangements. Some individuals consult for organizations in the hope that their work will eventu-

Table 7.1

Changes in Employment of Temporary Workers, 1982–1996

Year	Total payrolls (000)	Total temps (000)	% of total	Average hours/ week	Average hourly earnings ($)
1982	89,544	417	0.5	27.1	5.97
1986	99,344	837	0.8	31.1	6.65
1990	109,419	1,288	1.2	30.8	8.09
1995	117,203	2,189	1.9	31.8	8.79
1996	119,554	2,332	2.0	32.1	9.20

Source: U.S. Bureau of Labor Statistics.

ally result in full-time employment. Others consult for a number of companies at the same time to earn the equivalent of full-time pay; they choose this road because no single company needs their expertise on a full-time basis. While many consultants are self-employed, consulting is also an industry in and of itself. There is also a tradition in some fields of easing employees out of the workforce as retirement draws close; they work as consultants in areas in which they have gained very specific expertise that would be expensive to replace. Someone is brought in to take over most of the work they handled and to learn from them over time how to do the more specialized work. Since the downsizings of the late 1980s, many people have been called back to their old organizations on a consulting or independent contractor basis; they do the same work for about the same salary—but without benefits and with the understanding that the arrangement may be terminated at any time.

Box 7.1
The Travelers Corporation

In 1981, Travelers, a large financial services company in the area of insurance, health care, and investments, with headquarters in Hartford, Connecticut, began a job bank for its retirees. The program, named TravTemps, was eventually expanded to include other retirees as well as younger workers.

More than seven hundred employees are registered with TravTemps, which serves as an in-house temporary agency; about four hundred receive assignments every week. They are called in to replace workers who are on vacation or ill, and to help groups or departments trying to meet tight deadlines or deal with temporary work surges. They work at every level—from clerk to professional.

The company saves agency fees and avoids the extra paperwork involved in third-party arrangements while gaining the benefit of workers who need no introduction to the organization and its ways. The program also promotes diversity, debunking many myths about older workers, according to Donald DeWard, the head of the job bank, such as that older workers lack flexibility, are unable to learn new technologies, and often have difficulty working with younger employees. Travelers found in an internal survey that the retirees had no problem working in many locations for many different supervisors; they became computer-proficient through both formal courses and on-the-job training; and younger workers made special efforts to welcome them and view them as role models.

Source: Suzanne Crampton, John Hodge, and Jitendra Mishra, "Transition—Ready or Not: The Aging of America's Work Force," *Public Personnel Management* 25, no. 2, July 1996, pp. 243ff.; Jennifer J. Laabs, "What If They Don't Retire?" *Workforce* 76, no. 12, December 1997, pp. 54ff.; Commonwealth Fund, *The Untapped Resource* (New York: Commonwealth Fund, 1993), pp. 17–18; various stories in the business press.

Organizations prefer these kinds of arrangements because they allow them to add workers temporarily for specific projects while providing more stability than would be the case with temporary workers. This is particularly important when companies need to expand teams for special projects. In these situations, retired workers are often enticed to return for the duration of the project because they understand the corporate culture, thus ensuring that the project runs far more smoothly.

Individuals who work as consultants or contract workers for many different organizations incur the costs involved in marketing themselves, but the fees they charge usually take this into account. Older workers often find this road particularly stimulating. It allows them to pick and choose assignments, meet new people, and learn new things. In addition, they enjoy being treated as special and valuable. The choice of how much work to accept also helps to protect Social Security payments, which are reduced once earnings exceed a set amount.

Texas Refinery Corp., which is based in Fort Worth, Texas, hires older workers as independent contractors (as well as full-time). In 1995, five hundred of its three thousand–person sales force was past retirement age. The independent contractors who work for Texas Refinery receive commissions and benefits on the basis of their sales. Some of their retired workers have chosen this status because the part-time hours and flexible arrangements allow them to protect their Social Security by limiting the amount they earn to what is allowable before Social Security payments are cut. The company likes these arrangements because it believes that older salespeople have a distinct advantage in client relationships and that they are inclined to be self-starters.[4]

Telecommuting

Working at home has been gaining popularity in some companies in recent years: 5.4 million people worked at home at least three days a month in 1993; in 1998, 9.9 million did. For example, about 55 percent of managers at AT&T telecommute, but only 2 percent of Aetna employees do. At Leisure Co./America West, where 16 percent telecommute, potluck team dinners are held to make sure people keep in touch.[5]

These arrangements, which are made possible by advanced technology, are still taking shape, but it has become clear that while they offer many advantages, frequently they pose problems that need to be addressed by new rules of the road. For example, at-home work can make life easier for older employees if money is the major reason for returning to work. But working at home does not provide the social interaction that makes work so attractive for some older workers.

For younger workers who may rank home and family first, at-home work on a flexible schedule can provide the freedom to attend a child's school play or accomplish things more easily done during regular business hours, such as well-baby visits to the pediatrician. The elimination of commuting also means more hours at home with the family, especially important for those with young children whose bedtime often coincides with a parent's return from work. However, when such an arrangement is made early in a career, promotions tend to be a rarity. Many managers believe that those who choose to work at home are less involved in the company and its goals.

Telecommuting also can be problematic because of a lack of clear definition of performance expectations. Many telecommuters put in far too many hours, sometimes burning out because they are worried about the perceptions of peers and managers. Moreover, since they have no one to compare notes with, they find it hard to measure their own productivity. Managers are uncomfortable with long-distance oversight and worry about loss of control. To succeed, telecommuting arrangements take careful planning. It is critical to set regular hours and keep management, peers, and family aware of what they are. It also is important to have formal performance standards, to spend some time at the office on a regular basis, and always to be available for important meetings. At-home workers and telecommuters also must have a regular workplace that can be closed off from family living areas, and they need equipment that takes safety and ergonomics into account. Both managers and workers must have regular meetings to discuss goals and performance, and department meetings should be arranged so that telecommuters can attend in person at least some of the time.

On-call Work

On-call work often involves a guaranteed minimum number of hours. Organizations that must be fully staffed at all times in certain areas, such as hospitals, tend to make these arrangements. For the organization, it serves two purposes: It ensures that back-up personnel will be available at relatively low cost whenever needed and it provides an opportunity to find replacement workers. For some people, such work is seen as a road to developing an inside track to obtaining full-time work. For others, it eliminates some of the uncertainty of temporary work. Since on-call work usually requires working varying shifts, it is ideal for older workers who have few specific demands on their time. In hospitals, it often serves as a partial retirement strategy.

Special Retirement Options

Besides the varied work arrangements above that offer a range of possibilities for younger and older workers, other arrangements allow older workers to withdraw gradually from the workforce.

Experts such as Robert Friedland, the director of the National Academy on an Aging Society, in Washington, D.C., believe that, upon retirement, many boomers will "reconcile a dream of early retirement with their meager retirement savings. They'll compromise by trading in full-time, high-powered careers for less-stressful, part-time jobs. Such 'bridge jobs' will increase as more baby boomers hit their 50s and 60s."[6] Indeed, this trend is already beginning. As Susan MacManus reports, "Among workers 55 and older, 70 to 80 percent indicated an interest in part-time work, a job that would allow a day or two a week at home, and job sharing. These figures will grow as the population ages and technology permits more in-home work."[7]

Phased Retirement

Under phased retirement, workers close to ending their careers work out a plan for gradual withdrawal from the company. They reduce the number of days they work each week by, say, a day the first three months, then two days the next three, and so on until they reach full retirement. This benefits the organization because it allows for a transfer of the expertise and institutional knowledge of the retiring worker to the person who will eventually take over the job. The younger worker may actually job share with more than one person or have other responsibilities. This kind of job sharing matches older and younger employees rather than two workers who each want to work part of a week. Neuville Industries of Hildebran, North Carolina, set up a job-sharing program for employees over the age of sixty-two. The program, which was initiated in the early 1990s, is aimed at employees with at least five years of experience. It provides for job sharing with younger employees and allows employees to continue working for as long as they want. Moreover, these twenty-hour-a-week jobs come with benefits.[8]

Bridge Employment

In bridge employment, an older worker is often given special assignments, such as serving on a disaster recovery project or representing the company in a community project.

Seasonal Work

Under these arrangements, an older worker may agree to come back during the summer when many younger workers with children take vacation time. Because they know the company, they can quickly learn new specific tasks.

Work Abroad

Special assignments abroad are also proving a popular source of retirement work. Whirlpool Corp. finds it is less expensive to hire retired workers for short-term assignments abroad than to relocate full-time workers, Quaker Oats has tapped retirees for a project in Shanghai, and GTE also has tested this approach and plans to expand it.

Mentoring

To maintain their institutional history and values, and even some older skills and techniques, organizations often turn to older workers. Only those who worked in an organization for a long time can answer such questions as, Why did we choose that system when others were available? Why can't we get our foot in the door with company X? This information does not get captured in memos or expert systems; it is the stuff of history, stored in memory, recounted as conversation. One of the ways companies can capture this knowledge is to ask older workers to become mentors.

When asked about mentoring programs, Donna Martin of Pharmacia & Upjohn said that when she was at Baxter Health Care, "We were very proactively developing such programs because we really felt it would help younger workers and give them that benefit as well as give older workers a good sense of what added value they can bring."[9]

This new system of mentoring is close to the original Greek meaning of *mentor*—to teach—than to the more common business usage of facilitating someone's climb up the corporate ladder. In our booming economy, with unemployment under 5 percent, acquiring new skilled workers quickly poses a number of problems, because there are so few managers who are available and have the time to provide new employees with the training and supervision they need when starting out. A mentoring program can help fill the gap.

Making the Options Work

At the moment, these models are considered extensions of old solutions to workforce shortages. Companies must realize that these new models of work will not really add full value unless they are structured to provide fair salaries and benefits; that is, until corporate leaders recognize that these kinds of work arrangements are part of a new flexible model of work, they will not incorporate them into their organizational structure and develop sound policies for enforcing them.

The inequality in income and wealth of the past decades eased somewhat during the last couple of years of the 1990s as a result of extremely tight labor markets in a strong economy. Companies, however, must act now to set up policies to protect workers under the new model if the economy weakens; otherwise, disaffection from the corporate world will only intensify—with dire results when the boomers retire.

Training and Retraining

It is now clear to American workers that lifetime employment no longer exists. The question is, What will replace it? Peter Herriot, the director of research at Sundridge Park Management Centre in the United Kingdom, says that in the future, "big firms will have to offer the best professional workers regular opportunities to add to their marketable credentials in order to recruit or retain them."[10] Some companies have seen the light. The *Economist* says that "spending on corporate education has grown by 5% a year for the past decade." The $50 billion a year companies are now spending on "education and training . . . account for about half of America's total spending on higher education."[11] However, given corporate wealth, those numbers are not very impressive.

In the future, the willingness and ability to train and retrain workers, a cornerstone of the new social contract, is going to be a critical success factor in retaining workers. A survey conducted by the Hay Group, a Philadelphia-based management consultancy measuring worker commitment, found that the gap between committed employees (those planning to stay at least five years) and those planning to leave within the year was the largest when it came to their satisfaction with the opportunity they were given to learn new skills. A solid 61 percent of committed employees were satisfied with the opportunities to learn new skills provided by their current companies; only 25 percent of employees who planned to leave within the year were satisfied with such opportunities.[12]

Companies that want to be certain they have the kind of workforce they need, when they need it, will have to find ways to ensure that their employees participate in some form of continual education and training. There are many approaches they can take:

- On-the-job training, offering formal training programs in the workplace or at corporate learning centers, or making arrangements for employees to take courses, even earn degrees, at schools (from community colleges to universities, at the training centers of other organizations, or through online training programs)
- Apprenticeship systems that teach new skills in exchange for a commitment to work for the organization for a specified period of time

- Training to customize a worker's skills to suit the needs of the organization
- Education and training opportunities at the tail end of employment for specified periods of time, which would encourage workers to stay until projects are completed rather than search for a new position before the term of the contract is over
- Opportunities to move laterally across the organization so people are constantly challenged and learning.

On the surface, the greatest problem for companies is to shape the training programs that must be part of the new social contract to address the demands of all potential workers, no matter what their ages. (In practice, as we have seen, these differences turn out to be surprisingly unimportant.) Some companies are heavily engaged in such efforts; others are lagging. Some have hesitated to provide a great deal of training because they are afraid that their newly educated employees will take those skills elsewhere. Those fears could be eliminated by an examination of the experiences of Silicon Valley, which invests heavily in education, and the recently revived rust belt industries in Italy's Emilia-Romagna region, which believe in the benefits of industrial training cross-fertilization. In both areas, raising the level of employees' skills has benefited every company in the region.

Who Gets Trained?

At this time, companies that offer training do not usually do so across the board. Part of the reason is that the value of training is still measured in terms of the older models of work. According to those models, because employees settle into long-term employment after making two or three career moves, offering training to younger employees was considered a waste of resources. Those models also assumed that retirement would occur somewhere between age sixty-two and age sixty-five. Therefore, since nothing

Table 7.2

Hours of Training per Employee by Age, May–October 1995

Age	Hours of training		
	Total	Formal	Informal
24 and younger	24.1	2.7	31.1
25–34	46.5	14.0	32.5
35–44	45.7	15.4	30.3
45–54	56.2	17.2	39.0
55 and older	22.9	5.7	17.1

Source: U.S. Bureau of Labor Statistics.

changed very quickly in that model, there was only a limited value to training older workers in processes or methods that might not be fully implemented before they left. The amount of training given younger and older workers still follows this pattern; moreover, younger and older employees receive more of their training on an informal basis (see Table 7.2). In addition, surveys consistently show that most corporate educational efforts are overwhelmingly aimed at middle- and upper-level employees at managerial and professional levels.

Companies are going to have to change their ideas about who should receive training to match the realities of the new world of work. They would do well to follow the example of companies such as Oracle, Motorola, and Sun Microsystems that have developed huge education centers providing excellent training in advanced skills related to the technologies they produce to those inside—and outside—their organizations. Oracle in particular has recognized the need to make changes in response to the overall aging of the workforce, a fact made clear by the number of older workers sent to Oracle for training by the companies that buy Oracle's products (see Box 7.2).

Looking to the Bottom Line

Economists have long believed that companies receive the greatest return on the cost of training workers the longer they stay on the job. This reasoning is no longer valid. Today, training lasts only until new methods, systems, and processes appear. The amount of time a worker stays on the job is irrelevant. In fact, change is now such a constant that many predict that 80 percent of the population is likely to be left behind at some point in the next decade as industry after industry finds new ways to work.

In calculating retraining costs, time away from current jobs is taken into account, but time saved because retrained employees do not have to learn the ways of the company are not. Other often neglected costs are severance pay and recruitment efforts. The Corning Glass Company says it spends around $40,000 replacing each lost worker. Merck and Company says that training a replacement for a lost worker costs about one-and-one-half times that person's average salary. The productivity lost while a position is vacant, search fees for replacements, management time used for interviewing, and training time for the new hire add up to about $10,000 for about half of all companies and to more than $40,000 for 10 percent of companies. The more skilled the jobs, the higher the costs.[13]

Another issue is the cost of the loss of institutional memory

Box 7.2
Oracle Corporation

Headquartered in Redwood Shores, California, the Oracle Corporation is the world's second-largest software company, employing thirty-six thousand people. It is the leading supplier of software for enterprise information management and universally respected for the training it offers clients.

Like most major companies involved in information technology (IT), Oracle has a solid reputation for providing training. Its Oracle Education division is the second-largest IT training provider worldwide. Dedicated to providing customers and partners with superior technology training through traditional and emerging technology media, it has experienced a growth rate of at least 29 percent for five consecutive years.

In April 1998, it opened an Oracle Education Center in San Jose, California, bringing the number of education facilities it supports worldwide to three hundred, employing twelve hundred instructors. As part of its continuing need for employees versed in technology, it also launched a $50 million university training program, involving about a hundred universities.

Looking to the future, Oracle is preparing to address the issue of the current—and coming—worker shortfall. While most IT companies direct their training at young, inexperienced workers, Oracle is now targeting older workers, particularly at the Oracle Education Center, according to Klaus Andersen, vice president of global operations for Oracle's education division. The program is already meeting expectations, and the company is considering expanding the center.

Source: Malcolm Maclachlan, "Oracle Opens Worker Training Center," *TechWeb, the Technology News Site,* April 7, 1998; the business press; and author interviews.

when large numbers of employees are replaced because of the need for new skill sets. This problem is easily alleviated by retraining. Companies think this will not work because they believe that those with the most experience are least likely to accept retraining. While there is a degree of retraining burnout, most of it is a result of the amount of responsibility many older workers have, which makes freeing time for retraining extremely difficult. Older workers are also more likely to have experienced changes that did not make a difference. When companies explain the value of the new technology or process and help workers realize that the new skills they will gain will enhance employability, resistance is far less common. GTE Corporation provides a good example of the willingness of employees to embrace retraining (see Box 7.3).

Making Training Work

The fact that in the past corporate training has been focused on middle- and high-level employees and on those in their prime work years could be a stumbling block when younger and older workers alike are offered training under the new social contract. Trainers will have to keep in mind not only educational differences but generational differences and earlier learning experiences. They will have to modify their approaches in response. For example, older workers tend to do better with hands-on learning and have more problems with testing, but companies that have provided across-the-board training report little difference in training outcomes as a result of age.

The issue of retraining older workers in new skills is complicated by preconceived ideas about their ability and willingness to learn, especially when it comes to new technology. Sara E. Rix, senior policy adviser for AARP, points out that older workers are "caught up in a vicious cycle. Employers perceive them as less technologically adept than younger workers but also less likely to take steps to correct their shortcomings." For this reason, she

Box 7.3
GTE Corporation

GTE Corporation of Stamford, Connecticut, is one of the world's largest publicly held telecommunications companies and a leading provider of integrated telecommunications services. With 114,000 employees, this technology- centered organization has developed extensive training capabilities. Perhaps more important, that focus has made the entire organization learning-centered.

For example, in the late 1980s, GTE's Massachusetts operation was hit hard by major changes in the industry. Over the next eight years, their workforce was cut in half, from twelve thousand to six thousand, through downsizings. When more change was in the offing, the company realized it had to do something to stop the drain of employees who understood the company.

Dorothea R. Sparrow, who was then director of human resources for GTE Government Systems in Massachusetts, says that "GTE applied to the Department of Labor and was awarded $4 million for an eighteen-month retraining program for Massachusetts residents." (The company was allowed to extend the time line of the grant to twenty-four months.) She notes that the "aim of the program was to retrain the incumbent workforce . . . the people who were left. We had to get them up to par in the new way of thinking. We were no longer a government contractor. To survive, everyone had to become a sales person because we needed to get a lot of commercial business to replace the far larger government contracts we used to have."

Sparrow's first step was to contact a group of retirees who had elected to take a "voluntary out" program during the downsizings. They were members of a technical workforce, but "many agreed to come in on a volunteer basis." Although she used the grant money to bring in technical training firms and people from universities to give the courses, the volunteers did much of the planning and the evaluation of the training.

When the offer of retraining was made, acceptance was on a voluntary basis. Sparrow says the "participation level was phenomenal—about 70 percent, and half of the training was done on their own rather than the company's time." She says that "the participants were evenly split when it came to age—there were just as many people in their sixties as their forties and fifties."

Sparrow noted that success rates did not vary with age. She added that "most of the members of the workforce had graduate degrees and had kept their technological skills fairly current. Where they were lacking was in marketing and sales and the new software languages."

The ultimate goal, Sparrow added, was to "make those people who participated better qualified so that if positions came up as the company won new contracts and expanded, they would not have to find a new workforce."

Source: Author interview.

adds, they have a hard time keeping up "with new technology or other needed skills and consequently do become less relevant to their employers, who can then, with justification, accuse them of lacking" the skills those employers need.[14]

This situation may be easing, however. An AARP survey of human resources managers' ratings of older workers in terms of flexibility and comfort with new technology is revealing. The percentage of older workers rated "excellent" for flexibility rose from

28 percent in 1985 to 45 percent in 1994; when it came to comfort with new technology, it rose from 10 percent to 23 percent.[15] Since the older workers of 1985 had probably retired by 1994, it is clear that the rise is associated with the retirement of those who spent the least time with computers. If the trend continues, the baby boomers who are now forty-five to fifty should be totally comfortable with technology when they are older workers, which will ease the training challenge.

Those responsible for training also must distinguish between resistance to learning a new application or system and the ability to learn. In a world of frequent change, long hours, and constant pressure, the time demands of learning something new might be more the cause of resistance than fear of the technology. Those responsible for training must be sure that the following questions can all be answered yes:

- Has the need for the new system been explained in terms of the organization's business strategy and future goals?
- Has the workload of employees involved in skills training been adjusted to allow for training time?
- Do training schedules take concurrent initiatives into account?
- Is the training tailored to different learning styles?
- Is the relationship clear between the training curriculum and the trainees' job?
- Does the equipment used in technology training take ergonomics into account?

The costs of a shortage of skilled workers are too high to ignore. While enabling older workers constantly to upgrade their skills will help—if they are willing to stay on—training must become an integral part of every worker's life no matter what form his or her corporate attachment takes. Continual learning is the key to the future—for workers and for the corporations whose survival depends on their abilities.

Moreover, the responsibility for paying for training must be clearly set out in employment contracts. For example, contract employees needed for a twenty-month project could be hired under an arrangement that provides them with salary over twenty-two to twenty-four months, with the understanding that the last months will be a phaseout period involving paid training in a new skill set. This kind of arrangement is not only part of building a good reputation but in the end will provide more concrete value. First, most projects take longer to complete than originally estimated. Having a longer contract will provide the company with a grace period because someone under this kind of contract is less likely to plan to leave early. Second, if the company selects the kinds of skill training it offers in anticipation of its likely future skill needs, those receiving the training will be ready when the company that trained them needs them—and will be likely to sign up for another stint.

Enhancing more general skills is another issue. Employees working in teams often lack sufficient communications skills even though their technical skills and their skills in their area of expertise are well honed. There are a number of ways to approach this problem. Some companies provide tuition reimbursement for successful completion of appropriate courses at community colleges, but they expect their employees to take those courses on their own time. Others provide the training in-house on company time.

The point is not so much how this is all done but that it must be spelled out clearly in the hiring process. Workers will measure the importance a company puts on their future employability by its willingness to address this issue from the outset.

Diversity

Age discrimination might eventually disappear if the baby boomers' ability to change society at every stage of their lives continues.

However, even boomers will have a hard time making older "the in thing." In the workplace, the stumbling blocks are clear. A Society for Human Resource Management/AARP survey of managers found that while 32 percent of respondents said the issue of older workers was very important, "65 percent of the respondents said their organizations do not actively recruit older workers to fill open positions, and 55 percent said their organizations do not actively seek to retain workers who are 50 years old or older."[16] The myths about aging seem almost impossible to dispel.

In business the reality is that while age makes a difference in physical capacities, those differences do not make older workers less valuable. Sandra Winicur, an associate professor of biology at Indiana University South Bend who specializes in the physiological effects of aging, says that when it comes to "most of your physiological systems—kidneys, heart, circulatory system, muscular capacity, oxygen capacity—nothing may change in your day-to-day capacity to function through the mid-fifties, but your reserve capacity, the power you can call on in an emergency or a stressful situation, gradually diminishes for each system with time. For example, by age sixty, your total respiratory capacity and cardiac index is about 80 percent of what it is at age thirty, and it goes down another 10 to 40 percent over the next twenty years."

Winicur says that although this reserve capacity diminishes, "older people compensate ... learn to make adaptations that make them more able to put in a long day's work than when they were young. They don't assume they have eternal youth, so they pace themselves accordingly to avoid burning out." She notes that "when you are in your twenties, you can usually depend on bursts of energy and bursts of inspiration in a way that you probably can't in your fifties. A young person may be more free to procrastinate, to leave work for the last minute, to assume he or she can stay up all night, to assume he or she possesses the necessary energy for this. In your fifties you tend to know what your strengths are, what your weaknesses are, and most important, what your limits are. You are less likely to depend on bursts and on miracles, and you pace yourself much better. This makes it easier for other people to work with you and to depend on you."

Of course, she points out, the kind of work one does makes a huge difference: "If the work involves physical activity, you will see an effect much sooner than if the work involves mental activity. If it involves strong motor skills, the muscles tire sooner. If it involves fine motor skills, such as writing, you don't see an effect as soon" (see Box 7.4).

When it comes to learning, Winicur says that studies show there is little difference in total learning time until about the age of seventy in people who have continued to learn. She adds that "learning is a use-it-or-lose-it situation and someone who is used to learning new skills keeps open the pathways to learn new skills."

Winicur concludes that "in people who have been using their brains you see differences in mental ability after age sixty-five or seventy in speed of integration and coming up with the right word. But this is not a loss of ability, it is a slowing of ability, and while it may be important in some jobs, it may be totally irrelevant in others."[17]

Alexander Spence writes in *The Biology of Human Aging* that since "memory seems to be retained better in older persons who continue working or otherwise keep busy after retirement," companies should focus on retention of older workers rather than relying on their ability to recruit these workers when they have no other choice. He added that "it seems as if 'exercising' the brain helps to maintain its normal functioning" far longer.[18]

Dealing with the physical problems created by aging or stress requires:

- *Providing the right furniture.* Ergonomic surveys of computer stations are invaluable for all employees, because they help prevent repetitive strain injuries. For older workers, chairs should

Box 7.4
Philips Lighting Company

Kevin Doran, vice president of human resources and government and public affairs at Philips in Somerset, New Jersey, says that a large percentage of the people working at Philips "are engaged in manufacturing, and that probably presents more constraints on the kinds of accommodations you can make for an aging workforce. We do, however, have examples of success in individual cases, where sitting down in our unionized environment, we look at the issue and if someone is at the point where they cannot work productively with equipment because of its speed or the physical skills needed, we try to work out, based on their seniority, where else they could productively continue to contribute to the plant."

When it comes to retraining, Doran says the company has not found it necessary to take age into account. For example, Philips is currently moving to new enterprise software companywide that will affect all jobs. "Everyone is getting equal training regardless of their demographics. We don't see any difference in the ability to learn by age. People who want to learn are learning. We provide refresher and follow-up courses for those people, regardless of age, who don't get it the first or second time around. We also have remedial help on an individualized basis for those people who struggle." When asked if older workers were having a harder time with the training, Doran said they weren't. He added that "young or old, most of the time the mechanisms are there to do it, and also the technology has improved. Moreover, we have, in some cases, provided ways for people to practice off-line with no consequences until they feel comfortable with the way the new system affects their jobs."

> Doran adds that "Philips does sometimes call on people who have retired, who have good experience, and understand our business—and have indicated an interest in continuing their relationship with us—to consult on a per diem basis." Doran says that "enables the transfer of knowledge, allowing us to gain from their wonderful years of expertise and experience."
>
> *Source:* Author interview.

have arms to make it easier to rise with stiff joints; pillows can ease back strain; footrests can help circulation.

- *Stressing the importance of frequent minibreaks and stretching exercises.*
- *Checking the lighting in the workplace for adequacy and glare.* For older workers, computer screens often need adjustment to accommodate bifocals. Sometimes those who wear glasses only for reading or distance vision need special glasses for reading at the middle distance at which a computer screen is set.

In other words, there are actions that can help eliminate problems. Eliminating age prejudice will not be as easy but is possible. Part of the problem is that so much of this discrimination is subconscious, based on false assumptions, and reinforced daily by the media, particularly television and advertising.

Since age discrimination is the same as every other kind of prejudice, well-established diversity programs can be adopted to eliminate it. Of course, the place to start is at the top. Leaders must be forced to confront the problem. Demographic studies show that the current problem is only a forerunner of a larger problem that will hit hard in another few years. Human resource managers having a hard time finding applicants to fill jobs can use this information to help promote changes in policies that will facilitate attracting new hires. They also should take advantage of vacancies to bring home the need to keep older workers on the job. For example, if the order fulfillment department is having problems because of three empty slots due to early retirements, they must highlight the reason for the problem. Statements such as "If only Carol and Howard hadn't retired so early . . ." can begin to emphasize the need to keep people working longer.

Rewarding managers who retain older workers can have a strong impact, especially if those managers are then recruited as change agents. Circulating articles that highlight the contributions of older workers without stressing their age also is useful. So are workshops that make younger managers face and deal with their discomfort with older workers.

Paying the Price

Understanding and developing fair reward structures for the new models of work, putting in place training programs that build skills and employability for workers, and eliminating discrimination are all part of the new social contract. Together, they can help rebuild a trust in business that can combat current attitudes toward work, attitudes that have resulted in the withdrawal of many competent, productive workers. Businesses need these workers. Moreover, future economic stability may be adversely affected if early retirees end up barely making it later in life because they did not understand the realities of inflation and the probability of a very long life. The result will be too few workers and too few older people with adequate resources for their last years—a certain recipe for a downward economic spiral.

Chapter 8

Replacing Obstacles with Opportunities

The modern business system is at present more or less lawless, but the pressure of necessity during the next ten or twenty years will enforce its reform. Unless I wholly misinterpret the signs of the time, we are now in the morning hours of a period in which businessmen, in order to survive and succeed, will be compelled to adopt the sort of policies that will give us an increasingly better social order.

Edward A. Filene

Although Edward Filene's words ring very true today, Filene, a successful retailer, student of business, and philanthropist, wrote them in the mid-1920s.[1] The kinds of policies he was promoting then did not become a part of the American workplace until after World War II, and they were not put in place by individual businessmen. They were a result of actions taken by government, in large part as a result of the power of workers represented by unions, and they were made possible by a strong economy. Although those policies lasted almost half a century, conditions have changed dramatically since then. The problems those policies were addressing were created by the development of American manufacturing, a world of mass production and assembly lines, a workplace that was rigid and unchanging—where skills lasted a lifetime. The new world of work that has emerged today requires us once again to meet the challenge posed by Filene of adopting the "sort of policies that will give us an increasingly better social order."

Since one of the realities of the future will be the need to keep people interested in working longer, the new policies adopted must address the damage done during the transition to the new world of work during the last decades of the twentieth century. These new policies must ensure that the new workplace is profitable for both workers and businesses. These policies also must address the need for skilled knowledge workers, and they must face the issue of fair pay and access to the continual learning that workers need to keep up in a workplace where skill sets change rapidly and work is managed more by machines than by people. The unintended costs of such an effort must not be ignored, because they can change the future for which we are preparing.

Reaching agreement on which policies are needed and who will pay for them will be neither simple nor easy. The strongest player at the moment is business. This raises the question, What can workers do to make their voices heard in the debate between policymakers determined to push corporate leaders to act more in the interests of workers and corporate leaders who insist it is in everybody's interest for them to focus first on today's bottom line and tomorrow's new competition?

There Must Be a Simpler Solution

Some economists say that the labor pool is deeper than anyone realizes and that the actual withdrawal of older workers will not be as large as expected. Christopher Farrell of *Business Week* points out, in support of this position, that "the financial incentives to drop out of the workforce have weakened since the mid-1980s."[2] This will ease the problem of a worker shortfall but not eliminate it. These workers will need retraining because business has neglected its older workers on the assumption they would not remain at work for long. Moreover, the problem facing large corporations will not necessarily be solved because people stay at work longer. Because these large organizations face the continued resentment of workers who blame them for much of the turmoil in the late 1980s and early 1990s, they will not be employers of first choice for the working retired. In fact, it is likely that if those companies do not begin now to build the new social contract discussed in the last two chapters, the difference between enough workers and good enough workers is going to be a critical issue for them.

Farrell also discusses immigration as a possible solution, noting that the "rising levels of education in developing countries will make them more valuable as a source of workers."[3] The problem with depending on immigration to supply us with workers is that aging is a global phenomenon that could result in restrictions on the emigration of workers in the future, when those countries that might otherwise supply skilled workers are in the midst of their own crises caused by the graying of their populations.

Even if the current level of immigration is maintained, and many believe it should be lowered, the U.S. workforce will grow only 0.8 percent a year until 2006.[4] To make up the shortfall, we would have to open our doors even wider. In addition, since many of the workers we want would bring their families, the dependency ratio would increase further.

Another proposed solution is developing policies that encourage people to have more children. European nations such as France that are trying to halt their declining fertility rates offer families financial inducements to have more children—family allowances for second and third children as well as housing and schooling allowances—no matter how high the family's income.[5]

179

The best evidence that this approach does not work is from Sweden, which has the most family-friendly policies in the world, including more than a year of paid family leave after the birth of a child. Yet Sweden's fertility rate, which was hovering near replacement levels until 1990, began to fall precipitously after that, dropping to 1.6 in 1995. Then, as the faltering economy, which had been blamed for the tumbling rates, began an upswing, Swedish leaders hoped for an improvement. Those hopes were dashed over the next two years when the rate again tumbled—to 1.42.[6]

Since there is no way we can force people to have children, and incentives are largely ineffective, perhaps we need a social campaign to encourage people to move in this direction. However, given the time it would take for such a campaign to result in an increase in fertility rates and turn those children into the educated workforce we need in the unlikely event that the effort was effective, it would not solve the immediate problem, which will hit with full force in fewer than twenty years.

Doing It the Hard Way

Instead of endless discussions and a constant search for easy answers, what is needed is action. The first step is to find ways to retrain today's workers and ensure that the workers of tomorrow are educated in the basics and how to learn. The next step is to address the social and psychological costs of a model of work that does not provide benefits or equitable salaries. Following that, we need to examine the costs to older workers of remaining employed, given current pension policies, which were aimed at encouraging retirement rather than continued employment. Finally, we need to explore the issue of how employers and employees can achieve a balance of power in the context of the new model of work.

Learning . . . Again and Again

Specific skills will continue to change so rapidly that there is no way our schools can produce workers with the exact skills needed in the workforce tomorrow. Instead, our schools must produce literate workers with analytical skills. These future workers must learn how to update their skills on an ongoing basis, and they must be computer literate. This means improving our primary and secondary school system.

To start, business and government must wage a campaign to convince voters of the wisdom of supporting our nation's schools. Too many school bond votes indicate a lack of concern about the future. Here is where a public education campaign that clearly laid out the issue—Who will provide the goods and services you need tomorrow?—could be effective.

Government must be prepared to demand responsibility and accountability from parents and educators. New approaches must be tried—from education by for-profit enterprises to new school board arrangements to volunteers from corporate America teaching special skills—and the results carefully evaluated to determine what works and what doesn't. Then the information garnered must be used to rebuild our public schools so that they once again provide our nation's youth with the education they need to succeed in business and as citizens.

We also must provide people with the additional education they need at different times throughout their lives. A lifetime education allowance (such as the one proposed by the Clinton administration) is one road to consider; corporate-sponsored skill training centers in return for tax breaks is another. The problems of building and maintaining the kind of skilled workforce America needs is more than a social issue. Although business already plays a role in retraining people in advanced skills, it simply doesn't spend enough. As the twentieth century drew to a close, companies were investing an average of 1.5 percent of payroll on training, a number that must increase.[7]

The current policies that provide senior citizens with free tuition at public universities in some twenty states must be adjusted. If these programs change from life-enhancing courses for retirees to programs that provide work skills, corporations who benefit should have to bear at least some of the costs. In addition, private-public partnerships to provide training through community colleges need to be reviewed to ensure that the right parties are paying the bills. And the new world of distance learning must be evaluated to determine what value it provides to those already in the workforce.

Many possible roads can be taken so that all workers receive the necessary training to succeed, especially as they get older. Among them:

- *Training bonuses:* Payment and time off for courses that teach new skills. This could be approached as a reward for good performance.
- *New forms of accredited education:*
    1. Composite institutions accredited by the national or state governments that offer a large menu of choices. For example, 120 credits consisting of 40 at a traditional school (community, state college, or university), 40 at the equivalent of registered corporate universities, and 40 distance learning courses offered by any accredited school.
    2. New degree structures, such as a general degree certifying the completion of a program providing a liberal arts background as well as skills in research, statistics, and online expertise. This basic degree could have a skills component that was time bound and had to be renewed periodically. It would be the equivalent of updating the old BA every five years by the addition of new courses in the major area of study. Those "update" credits could be obtained through the original university, perhaps through extension courses, corporate training courses, and so forth.
- *Reimbursement:* Making the cost of retraining the unemployed a part of unemployment insurance in all states.

A Fair Day's Pay

In 1995, 29.4 percent of workers had moved to nonstandard work arrangements. Unfortunately, these jobs do not pay as well as similar, full-time jobs requiring the same qualifications. Moreover, only 12 percent of such jobs offer employer-provided health care, while a little over 66 percent of standard jobs do.[8]

The issue of salaries and benefits for nontraditionally structured work presents a number of difficulties. Every job comes with a set of fixed and variable costs. Fixed costs, which account for about 20 percent of the total cost of a worker to a company, include training, hiring, and health insurance; variable costs, which account for about 77 percent, include wages and salaries, pensions, paid vacations, and certain contributions to government programs such as FICA, unemployment insurance, and workman's compensation.

The current system creates a number of problems for older workers. For example, the fixed costs for older workers are higher, mostly owing to the costs of their medical insurance. In the past, such fixed costs for older workers as recruitment and training also were higher because they were amortized over a shorter period than for younger workers. Today, job tenure is far shorter across the board, changing the equation.

The complexity of this issue involves such things as setting salaries for part-time workers who share a single job. If each is paid half the salary and full benefits, the costs of that job rise when it is shared. As a result, many companies who provide such benefits reduce salaries to accommodate the extra expense—although some deal with it by sharing the costs of the benefits with workers. Another complication is that today the rules governing less-than-full-time contingent work and contract work are tightening, making it harder for companies to maintain that someone in such a position for a long time is not entitled to benefits. These issues are in flux, and the courts and legislation will help set rules.

When constructing the new, flexible model of work, employers must understand that it is not only full-time, permanent employees who deserve adequate compensation. That may have been a defensible position when those jobs were the norm and anyone granted a special arrangement was expected to pay something for the privilege. The change in the norm requires revisiting the whole question of fair and equitable compensation.

Easing the Penalties of New Work Arrangements

Not only employers penalize those pursuing new models of employment. At the moment, the structure of some government policies tends to keep people out of the workforce. For example, Social Security benefits are reduced for those who earn above a certain amount; in 1997, retirees under seventy lost one dollar for every three dollars they earned over $13,500. Those over seventy are not subject to the earnings test.

In addition, company pensions often are affected by earnings if an employee continues to work after a certain age, say, sixty. According to David Durham, assistant vice president of benefits for CIGNA, the Philadelphia-based corporation has a program for its retirees known as Encore that hires retirees on a temporary basis. These former employees, however, are limited to eighty hours a month of work because after that their pensions are affected on a month-by-month basis.[9]

Moreover, companies and employees must begin to look toward portable pensions and portable health insurance coverage, perhaps through unions, trade associations, or even government, if current workers are going to achieve adequate retirement incomes. Models for such a system can be found in the world of higher education and in the entertainment industry. For example, teachers and others associated with educational institutions are all covered by a pension plan, TIAA-CREF, in which they remain as they shift

184

from institution to institution. The entertainment industry has unions, such as the Writers Guild of America West, that provide health care and pension plans to their members—who rarely work for a single employer for any length of time.

The problem of health coverage for all citizens is one the government has long been debating but seems a long way from solving. Almost forty million Americans were without health benefits as the twenty-first century began. Older workers who leave full-time employment to work part-time can lose their health benefits if they work less than a certain number of hours. In addition, older workers face a particularly difficult set of issues when switching companies or attempting to work part-time. Because they often have preexisting conditions (which do not in any way affect their ability to work), when they switch insurers they are not covered for those conditions for a stipulated period of time—often two years.

A Strong Voice at the Table

In 1954, 38 percent of workers in the private sector were members of labor unions; today, that figure is 11 percent, and shrinking. Some fear this change, noting that the inequality of wealth and income in America has grown to staggering proportions; others cheer it, believing that unions reduce the competitiveness of American business in a world marked by intense global competition.

When skilled workers and craftsmen of the agricultural era joined together for their own protection against employers' demands, they formed craft unions centering on their skills. These unions were communities of individuals that jointly set the rates employers would have to pay to hire them.

With the advent of mass production, this all changed. Large plants built to produce goods by machine developed hierarchical structures, placing a layer called "management" between workers and employers that determined how much workers would do in a day, how they would do it, and what they would be paid. Negotiating with these new "bosses" was far more difficult, particularly since the work being done in these large plants involved people with many different types of skills, who therefore belonged to many different groups. The result was the formation of large unions that had the clout to engage in collective bargaining from a position of strength.

In recent years, this arrangement has been falling apart because the world of work has once again changed. This time, the change involves both the structure of the large organizations that employ workers and the nature of the work that most people do. The service sector is a confusing amalgam of messengers and management gurus, sales clerks and stockbrokers, broom pushers and brain surgeons. For various reasons, including the perception of the service sector as more white collar than blue in its composition, unions have never played a large role in this sector.

It may be time for workers to band together once again, but in new ways. Groups of workers might join under umbrella organizations that represent those with a particular set of skills. Nelson Lichtenstein, a professor of political science at the University of Virginia, suggests that given today's flexible organizations, "American unions need to explore a more flexible organizing model, such as those in the building and garment trades, where for over a century local unions have operated upon a wide variety of principles: craft, ethnic, regional, and industrial."[10]

One piece of legislation needs revisiting to lay the groundwork for such new forms of worker associations. The National Labor Relations Act does not guarantee associational rights to high-skill autonomous or semiautonomous workers who perform managerial or supervisory work. In the new world of work, such responsibilities have been placed in the hands of workers across the organization because of changes brought by technology and teamwork. Is a team leader who prepares a team's progress reports a supervisor, even if no one in the company reports directly to him? And is every worker a manager in flattened organizations?[11]

Since it is unlikely that any individual can stand up to a company and win, the American worker needs to find a way to establish a position from which to bargain. However, reaching agreement on what kind of representation workers need is not going to be accomplished quickly.[12] American workers need to find effective ways to deal with the businesses that employ them. Exploring options for strengthening their voice is a way to start. American business must look back at the last major change in the world of business—the advent of manufacturing—and remember that unions were formed out of worker anger and resentment about workplace conditions. Meetings of representatives from both sides should explore whether formal representation is once again necessary and what forms such representation should take.

There's Always Something

Since every change brings other changes, it is important to keep in mind all the possible economic and social consequences of full employment at ever-later stages of life. For many years now, our nation has been encouraging volunteerism. We have tried to build a volunteer workforce that receives its rewards in the form of personal satisfaction. A large part of that new volunteer workforce was built of retirees when women, who had long filled that role, moved into the paid workforce. If retirees return to the office, who will replace them? And if we don't find replacements, who will suffer?

Another unintended consequence concerns the retirement communities built in warmer climates to accommodate retirees. What will happen to those homes and the communities in which they have been built if people work longer or, because they are working retired, decide to remain in the homes they have always lived in? Since people also live longer, these retirement communities may continue to serve their current purpose, but because they

187

are likely to have a larger population of the oldest old, caretaking may pose a dilemma.

Who Will Be There to Help?

The longer people remain in the workforce, the better it will be for the economy. Or will it? When women entered the workforce in large numbers, our nation found itself facing a lack of volunteers in all sorts of areas, especially during normal working hours. As a result, volunteer organizations turned to the expanding group of retiring workers and the response was wonderful.

The value of retirees' work is enormous. The Commonwealth Fund estimated that the "time that older Americans spend helping sick or disabled family members and friends is equivalent to the hours of 3.4 million full-time caregivers." Multiplying those hours by $5.60, the amount earned by those doing similar work, the worth of the work provided by those unpaid caregivers is $40 billion a year. Moreover, older people also provide a great deal of help to their families, often by taking care of their grandchildren during working hours. The value of that care is "equivalent to the hours of 7.7 million full-time childcare workers. At an hourly rate of $3.35, their unpaid assistance . . . is worth $48 billion a year." Those numbers should be put in perspective: The Medicare budget for home health benefits in 1993 was about $7 billion; the Head Start program was allocated less than $3 billion.[13]

The kind of help provided by older volunteers is going to be very difficult to replace in many sectors. As Emily Vallelong, the administrative director of Volunteer Services for the Sisters of Charity/St. Vincent's Campus, New York City, says, "Volunteers do the work that the staff is just too busy to get to. For instance, messenger service. Our volunteers go around the hospital delivering a variety of different things, X-ray reports, blood specimens to the laboratory. They field the calls that come in to the medical center. In June 1998, we fielded 4,174 in-house telephone calls to the

messenger service, which resulted in some 13,000 messenger runs."
She said that the hospital has almost seven hundred volunteers on
the rolls in any given year and the program saved St. Vincent's
more than $1 million over the year. Although a surprising number
of these volunteers are in their eighties, most are far younger, recent
retirees.[14]

Shifting Sands

In 1996, seniors contributed $307 million in benefits to Arizona's
economy, not counting $23 billion in consumer spending. In states
with large populations of seniors—for example, Florida, Arizona,
California—retirees are a growth industry that affects home building, hospitals, restaurants, and shopping malls.[15] The idea that
people will no longer withdraw from the workforce and move to
these enclaves is worrisome to states that depend on revenue from
property taxes as well as taxes paid by the people who provide the
services to these communities. Of course, they also worry about
the consequences of huge numbers of these citizens getting much
older and needing care that they cannot afford.

On the other hand, there are no guarantees that, if retirement
continued to mean withdrawal from work, the Sunbelt would
continue to flourish, with new retirees coming in to replace older
ones. It would not be surprising if the baby boomers once again
asserted their differences from the generation that came before
them. Indeed, there are already indicators that boomers want a
more active lifestyle and prefer more exciting activities than their
parents did at comparable ages.

Many boomers who are planning to retire are already buying
homes for that period of their lives, but they are choosing communities closer to their present homes. Martha Moyer, a spokeswoman
for Del Webb Corp., a developer of retirement communities that
has begun to focus on the North, building communities in states
such as Pennsylvania and New Jersey, says that while earlier retire-

ment is continuing, it is a different type of retirement, marked by part-time work, and the choices of places to retire are made on a different basis. "People want to remain near their workplaces," she said.[16]

The effects of the boomers' economic choices will be unavoidable, and, although it would be useful to predict exactly what those choices will be, no one is likely to do so with any degree of reliability.

Act Now

American history is rife with stories of those who achieved success through the conquest of new frontiers because they had the energy and strength to withstand hardship. As we move into a new world, we have become a nation whose median age is about triple what it was when we were founded. But although we are an older nation, the new frontiers we are exploring today require energy of the mind, not physical energy—and that kind of energy defies age.

Business leaders might heed some additional words of wisdom imparted by Edward Filene and ignored by his peers in 1926:

> *The successful businesses of the future will be the businesses that improve the processes and reduce the costs of production, rid distribution of its present indefensible wastes, bring the price of the necessities of life lower and lower, shorten the hours of labor and enlarge the margin of leisure, eliminate periodic depressions and recurrent unemployment, limit the area of the industrial battlefield and enlarge the floor space of the council chamber, create better and better working conditions, pay higher real wages, and increase the comfort and prosperity of both their employees and their customers.*[17]

Business leaders have re-created the world of work and won great personal rewards through actions in keeping with Filene's first two suggestions. Now, it is time for them to complete the list of suggestions, for they are, as is the title of the book in which Filene's words appeared, *The Way Out.*

Conclusion: Muscle, Machine, Mind

Work in America has been undergoing profound changes. Employment has moved from farm to factory floor to desktop, and the power needed to accomplish work has moved from muscle to machine to mind. Each of these changes has been brought about by developments in technology made possible by advances in human knowledge. Each new stage came at a comfortable high point in the previous stage and caused enormous disruptions that brought unhappiness and dislocation to many.

As the machine age began to take hold in the early twentieth century, agriculture as a source of jobs, which reached its peak in 1850, began to decline as a result of increasing efficiencies brought by mechanization. Those displaced from farms turned to the new factories built to produce goods that made life easier and better. Workers found themselves dealing with a world of work that demanded they move indoors, spending a large part of their lives tied to one place, doing the same thing over and over alongside other workers involved in the same process. The model of work that developed as mass production first took hold was, like farm work, rigid and taxing. Machines increased productivity, but factory work made draining physical demands. As time went by, machines improved and work began to demand more mental skills.

Once again, midcentury marked a high point, but in 1950 it was a high point in manufacturing, and once again it marked the beginning of a profound change. The technological advances and the onset of globalization in the following decades means that now, in 2000, the workplace is again in a state of flux. This time, however, the change is more subtle. The switch from farm to factory meant a change both in employers and place of employment; it was a clean break that allowed the construction of a new model of work. The switch from factory to desktop has not been as clearcut; employers often remain the same and so does the idea of place. At this time, we can only predict the outlines of the high point of this cycle, which should, if the past is any indication, hit about 2050.

Examining these changes through a series of snapshots in time is useful:

In 1850, the average American worker was in his early twenties, doing hard physical labor on a farm. He worked until he died, but the contribution he made changed over the years from purely physical work to include counseling and advice based on experience.

In 1900, the average worker was in his mid-twenties and searching for employment because farm work had become harder and harder to find. He and hundreds of thousands of workers like him moved into the mills and factories that were becoming increasingly a part of the American landscape, but it was neither a comfortable nor secure life. Most people worked until they died.

In 1950, the average American worker was in his early thirties and worked with machines in a factory, where he remained for another thirty years and then retired. Over the years, he learned how to run a number of different, new machines. Some workers with good educations and skills joined the ranks of white-collar workers, putting their experience on the shop floor to work managing the people on the factory floor; they worked until they retired.

In 2000, the average American worker is a man or woman in his or her late thirties, working for a company that uses technology to enhance its employees' ability to produce, sell, and distribute products and/or services. The workplace, which has been changing constantly, is in the midst of what might be yet another evolution—to electronic business—and what retirement will mean is very uncertain.

Looking ahead, the next snapshot may look like this:

In 2050, the average worker is likely to be a man or woman in his or her forties, working from wherever he or she happens to be at a given time to produce creative and innovative services. These knowledge workers connect with co-workers and clients through technology. Former corporate centers are now used as occasional meeting places and training centers for learning the latest technologies. These workers will work until they die—but they will take time away from work throughout their lives to pursue additional education, travel, or devote themselves to family.

These snapshots help to answer the question, How can corporate America survive the graying of the workforce? The changes in the kind of work Americans do and the abilities needed to do it mean that time and place are becoming irrelevant. A company will soon have no central location other than a small headquarters. In this world of work, knowing how to learn and how to handle change is critical, for it is a world in which businesses are constantly adapting to new market demands. In this world, workers who can provide innovative and creative ideas for new products and services, most of which will be produced in less-developed nations, are what is important. In this world of work, age simply doesn't matter—age, any age, works.

Is it that simple? Of course not. The road from 2000 to 2050 will not be a smooth one. It will take a concerted effort on the part of business, government, labor, academia, policymakers, and citizens to make this happen, just as getting from 1900 to 1950 took a huge effort. Keep in mind that each time a new cycle of change begins to tear apart the current arrangements, the doomsayers strike: In the 1960s, there were warnings that we faced a world of too much leisure where work would occupy little time and people would struggle to find ways to fill their lives; now some are warning that the end of work is upon us as technology replaces all workers, leaving people with no way to earn enough to support themselves. Predictions such as these might be worth thinking about were it not for the fact that these technologies are created, built, maintained, and advanced by people. Instead of fretting and fuming about the disasters that the doomsayers predict, we must start today to make the changes that will solve the problems we are facing. As H.G. Wells said in 1901, "The past is but the beginning of a beginning."

Notes

Unless otherwise noted, the demographic data throughout are drawn from various publications and online materials of the Census Bureau and the Bureau of Labor Statistics, especially the *Historical Statistics of the United States* (published by the U.S. Department of Commerce, Bureau of the Census); Kevin Kinsella and Yvonne J. Gist, *Older Workers, Retirement, and Pensions: A Comparative International Chartbook* (1995); U.S. Census Bureau, *Population Projections of the United States by Age, Sex, and Hispanic Origin: 1995 to 2050,* which is available on the Internet at http://www.census.gov/prod/www/titles.html#popest; various releases found on the Bureau of the Census's web site at www.census.gov as well as from publications, especially news releases, of the Bureau of Labor Statistics, which can be accessed at http://stats.bls.gov:80/newsrels.htm.

Much of the general information contained throughout this book is a result of my years as a vice president of The Century Foundation, formerly the Twentieth Century Fund, a New York–based research organization that has been exploring various aspects of the issues surrounding the aging of America. I have been a participant in that work and have access to data collected for the foundation's programs in this area. Our focus on Social Security, which has resulted in dozens of publications over the past few years, is reflected in our web site devoted to this issue and can be explored at www.socsec.org.

Notes

The quotations that head the chapters, unless otherwise identified, are culled from discussions in group settings undertaken in the course of consulting assignments, including a series of sessions devoted to improving communications skills conducted for a major financial printer in 1997, a large benchmarking project for a hospital in 1996, and a change management program for an insurance company in 1995. Sometimes the comments overlapped, with various individuals finishing sentences for one another. Some remarks were the result of discussions of this issue with small groups assembled for that purpose. Those interviewed were baby boomers; more were older than younger boomers.

Introduction

1. General statistics are, as indicated in the general introduction to the notes, from government sources, specifically in this case, from a news release jointly published by the Bureau of Labor Statistics and the Bureau of the Census. The information is available online at http://www.bls.census.gov/cps/pub/empsit_0399.htm (accessed 7-3-99).
2. Organisation for Economic Co-operation and Development, *Maintaining Prosperity in an Ageing Society* (Paris: OECD, 1998), p. 124.
3. Commonwealth Fund, *The Untapped Resource: The Final Report of the Americans over 55 at Work Program* (New York: Commonwealth Fund, 1993), p. 28.
4. Gene Koretz, "Quick to Hire and Quick to Fire," *Business Week,* May 31, 1999, p. 34.

Chapter 1

1. Michael Specter, "Population Implosion Worries a Graying Europe," *New York Times,* July 10, 1998, p. A6.
2. Ibid.

3. Paul Yakoboski and Jennifer Dickemper, "Increased Saving but Little Planning: Results of the 1997 Retirement Confidence Survey," *EBRI Issue Brief,* November 1997, p. 4.
4. Greg Gillespie, "Compensation Trend: Not Just a Paycheck," *The Institute,* November 1996, available at http://www.institute.ieee.org/ INST/nov96/comp.html (accessed 7-18-99).

Chapter 2

1. Fernando M. Torres-Gil, *The New Aging: Politics and Change in America* (New York: Auburn House, 1992), pp. 12–15.
2. Andrea Stone, "Not Boomers, Not Xers, They Are Tweeners," *USA Today,* March 22–24, 1996, p. A1.
3. Susan MacManus, *Young v. Old: Generational Combat in the 21st Century* (Boulder, Colo.: Westview Press, 1996), p. 10.
4. Cheryl Russell, *The Master Trend: How the Baby Boom Generation Is Remaking America* (New York: Plenum Press, 1993), p. 17.
5. Bruce Tulgan, *Work This Way* (New York: Hyperion, 1998), p. 17.
6. Paul Yakoboski and Jennifer Dickemper, "Increased Saving but Little Planning: Results of the 1997 Retirement Confidence Survey," *EBRI Issue Brief,* November 1997, p. 4.
7. Aon Consulting, *America@Work* (Chicago: Aon Consulting, 1998), p. 9.
8. Richard Miniter, "Generation X Does Business," *American Enterprise,* July/August 1997. At http://www.theamericanenterprise.org/genx.htm (accessed 5-28-99).
9. MacManus, *Young v. Old,* p. 11.
10. Catalyst released an important study of this issue in 1997: "A New Approach to Flexibility: Managing the Work/Time Equation." Information about Catalyst and how to purchase this and other publications is available on the Internet at www.catalystwomen.org.
11. Watson Wyatt, "Aging Workforce Emerges as Concern for Employers Worldwide," press release, Bethesda, Md., March 3, 1998. At

http://www.watsonwyatt.com/homepage/Pres_Rel/Mar98/aging.htm (accessed 6-16-98).

Chapter 3

1. Aaron Bernstein, "We Really Want You to Stay. Really," *Business Week,* June 22, 1998, p. 72.
2. New York Times, *The Downsizing of America* (New York: Times Books, 1996), p. 18.
3. Gene Koretz, "Downsizing's Painful Effects," *Business Week,* April 13, 1998, p. 23.
4. Bureau of Labor Statistics at http://stats.bls.gov:80/news.rel/disp.nws.htm (accessed 9-25-98).
5. Edward N. Wolff, *Top Heavy: The Increasing Inequality of Wealth in America and What Can Be Done About It,* a Twentieth Century Fund Report (New York: New Press, 1996), pp. 72–73.
6. Michael Barone, *Our Country: The Shaping of America from Roosevelt to Reagan* (New York: Free Press, 1990), pp. 163–64.
7. Paul Osterman, *Securing Prosperity: The American Labor Market: How It Has Changed and What to Do About It,* a Century Foundation Book (Princeton, N.J.: Princeton University Press, 1999), chapter 5.
8. Barone, *Our Country,* p. 166.
9. Otis Port, "Swan Song for Laissez-Faire?" *Business Week* (special issue, "Innovation"), 1989, p. 174.
10. David I. Levine, *Reinventing the Workplace: How Business and Employees Can Both Win* (Washington, D.C.: Brookings Institution Press, 1995), p. 5.
11. Robert J. Crawford, "Reinterpreting the Japanese Economic Miracle," *Harvard Business Review,* January-February 1998, p. 180.
12. Jon R. Katzenbach and Douglas K. Smith, *The Wisdom of Teams: Creating the High-Performance Organization* (Boston: Harvard Business School Press, 1993), p. 15.
13. See Beverly Goldberg and John G. Sifonis, *Dynamic Planning: The*

Art of Managing Beyond Tomorrow (New York: Oxford University Press, 1994), for a detailed examination of companies' problems with the advent of technology.

14. "The Case of the Disappearing Costs," *Business Week,* July 20, 1998, p. 6.

15. Hammer, with coauthor James Champy, expanded the article into a book, *Reengineering the Corporation: A Manifesto for Business Revolution* (New York: HarperBusiness, 1994), that quickly became a best-seller.

16. Lisa Baggerman, "The Futility of Downsizing," *Industry Week,* January 18, 1993, p. 27.

17. Charles Heckscher, *White-Collar Blues* (New York: Basic Books, 1995), p. 4.

18. U.S. Department of Labor, Bureau of Labor Statistics, Current Employment Statistics Survey and Current Population Survey; U.S. Department of Commerce, Bureau of the Census, *Historical Statistics of the United States, Colonial Times to 1970,* Part I (Washington, D.C.: Government Printing Office, September 1975), p. 138.

19. Stephen A. Herzenberg, John A. Alic, and Howard Wial, *New Rules for a New Economy: Employment and Opportunity in Postindustrial America,* a Twentieth Century Fund Book (Ithaca, N.Y.: Cornell University Press, 1998), pp. 23 and 27, Tables 3 and 4.

20. Federal Reserve Bank of Cleveland, "Labor Markets," in *Economic Trends,* April 1996, at http://www.clev.frb.org/research/apr96et (accessed 7-18-99).

21. Ronald J. Alsop, ed., *The Wall Street Journal Almanac, 1998* (New York: Ballantine Books, 1998), p. 242.

22. John J. Keller, "AT&T to End Year with Same Size Work Force," *Wall Street Journal,* December 30, 1996, p. 43.

23. Louis Uchitelle, "More Downsized Workers Are Returning as Rentals," *New York Times,* December 8, 1996, p. 34.

24. Bruce Nussbaum, "Downward Mobility," *Business Week,* March 23, 1992, p. 59.

25. Kenneth Labich, "The New Unemployed," *Fortune,* March 8, 1993, p. 40.
26. Susan Caminiti, "What Happens to Laid-off Managers," *Fortune,* June 13, 1994, p. 68.
27. David M. Gordon, *Fat and Mean: The Corporate Squeeze on Working Americans and the Myth of Managerial "Downsizing"* (New York: Free Press, 1996), pp. 56–57.
28. Peter Cappelli et al., *Change at Work* (New York: Oxford University Press, 1997), p. 38.
29. Hedrick Smith, *Rethinking America* (New York: Random House, 1995), p. 410.

Chapter 4

1. Dora L. Costa, *The Evolution of Retirement: An American Economic History, 1880–1990* (Chicago: University of Chicago Press, 1998), pp. 27–28.
2. Ken Dychtwald and Joe Flower, *Age Wave: The Challenges and Opportunities of an Aging America* (New York: Bantam Books, 1990), pp. 32–33.
3. Peter G. Peterson, *Gray Dawn: How the Coming Age Wave Will Transform America—and the World* (New York: Times Books, 1999), p. 40.
4. Costa, *The Evolution of Retirement,* p. 11.
5. Kenneth G. Manton, Larry S. Corder, and Eric Stallard, "Monitoring Changes in the Health of the U.S. Elderly Population: Correlates with Biomedical Research and Clinical Innovations," *FASEB Journal,* October 1997, p. 923.
6. Detailed information about the Social Security program is available from The Century Foundation, particularly from its Social Security web site (www.socsec.org) and a series of issue briefs, papers, and books it publishes on this subject. Among the most important books it has released are Henry J. Aaron and Robert D. Reischauer's

Countdown to Reform, Robert Ball's *Straight Talk about Social Security,* and *Beyond the Basics: Social Security Reform,* edited by Richard C. Leone and Greg Anrig, Jr.

7. U.S. Senate Committee on Labor and Human Resources, *Is Working America Preparing for Retirement?,* hearing before the Subcommittee on Aging, 104th Cong., 2d sess., June 13, 1996, S.Hrg. 104–508. Comments of Senator Barbara Mikulski, p. 3.

8. William G. Gale, "Are Americans Saving Enough for Retirement?" A Century Foundation Report, New York, December 1998, pp. 20, 22.

9. "Passing the Buck," *Economist,* May 15, 1999, p. 78.

10. The personal savings rate, low in comparison with that in other nations, has steadily declined for decades. Compiled by U.S. Department of Commerce, Bureau of Economic Analysis, the pattern can be seen at http://www.asec.org/perssav.htm (accessed 12-9-98).

11. Laurence J. Kotlikoff, *Generational Accounting: Knowing Who Pays, and When, for What We Spend* (New York: Free Press, 1992), pp. 57–58.

12. Gale, "Are Americans Saving Enough for Retirement?" p. 20.

13. Paul Yakoboski, Pamela Ostruw, and Jennifer Hicks, "What Is Your Savings Personality? The 1998 Retirement Confidence Survey," *EBRI Issue Brief Number 200* (Washington, D.C.: Employee Benefit Research Institute, August 1998), p. 8.

14. Paul Yakoboski and Jennifer Dickemper, "Increased Saving but Little Planning: Results of the 1997 Retirement Confidence Survey," *ERBI Issue Brief Number 191* (Washington, D.C.: Employee Benefit Research Institute, November 1997), p. 12.

15. Ken Dychtwald, *Age Power: How the 21st Century Will Be Ruled by the New Old* (New York: Jeremy P. Tarcher/Putnam, 1999), p. 98.

16. Philip Kotler and Eduardo L. Roberto, *Understanding Social Marketing: Strategies for Changing Public Behavior* (New York: Free Press, 1989), p. 6.

17. These events are brilliantly chronicled in Sherna Berger Gluck's *Rosie the Riveter Revisited: Women, the War, and Social Change*

(New York: Meridian, 1988) and Penny Coleman's *Rosie the Riveter* (New York: Crown, 1995).

18. Gluck, *Rosie the Riveter Revisited,* p. 261; also see chapters 1 and 12 for an interesting analysis of the phenomenon of social change and its unintended consequences.

19. William Symonds, "Far From the Tour-Bus Crowds," *Business Week,* July 20, 1998, p. 102.

20. Author interview, December 4, 1998. Ms. Vallelong, who has worked with the hospital volunteer program for fifteen years, was an invaluable guide to the motives of the volunteers and the effects of volunteering on older people. Information she provided on the financial impact of volunteers on the hospital appears in chapter 9.

21. Jimmy Carter, "The Best Years of Our Lives," *Business Week,* July 20, 1998, p. 113.

22. Dennis Berman, "Late Blooming Scholars," *Business Week,* July 20, 1999, p. 106.

23. Cynthia Thomas, "Making the Grade," *Wall Street Journal Interactive Edition,* September 14, 1998, at http://interactive3.wsj.com/public/current/articles/SB90536805880002250.htm (accessed 7-5-99).

24. Kevin Sack, "Older Students Bring New Life to Campuses," *New York Times,* March 21, 1999, Section 15, p. 8.

25. Eric Hubler, "The New Faces of Retirement," *New York Times,* January 3, 1999, Section 3, p. 1.

26. Melissa Levy, "Job Seniority," *Star Tribune* (Minneapolis), October 5, 1997, p. 1D.

27. Stan Hinden, "We're Retired—When We're Not at Work," *Washington Post,* December 13, 1998, p. H1.

Chapter 5

1. "The Big Picture," *Business Week,* December 14, 1998, p. 8.
2. Mike McNamee, "First Hired, First Fired?" *Business Week,* August 17, 1998, p. 22.

3. Tony Horwitz, "Some Who Lost Jobs in Early '90s Recession Find a Hard Road Back," *Wall Street Journal,* June 26, 1998, pp. A1, A9.

4. See Edgar H. Schein, *Organizational Culture and Leadership* (San Francisco: Jossey-Bass, 1985), pp. 1–12, for a discussion of this concept.

5. Public Law 90-202.

6. The U.S. Equal Employment Opportunity Commission (EEOC) provides this information on its web site at http://www.eeoc.gov/stats/adea.html (accessed 12-18-98).

7. Quoted in Marilyn Gardner, "For More Americans, Retiring Includes Clocking in for Work," *Christian Science Monitor,* November 14, 1997, p. 10.

8. Susan S. Meyers, ed., "Creativity and Productivity: Not Age Specific Characteristics," Minnesota Extension Service, Special Research Report, September 1991. At http://www.cyfc.umn.edu/Document/G/B/GB1003.html (accessed 12-21-98).

9. Watson Wyatt, "Aging Workforce Emerges as Concern for Employers Worldwide," press release, Bethesda, Md., March 3, 1998. At http://www.watsonwyatt.com/homepage/PresRel/Mar98/aging.htm (accessed 6-16-98).

10. Charlene Marmer Solomon, "Unlock the Potential of Older Workers," *Personnel Journal* 74, no. 10, October 1995, pp. 56–66.

11. SAIF Corporation, "The Graying of the Baby-boomers: Facing Up to an Aging Workforce," May 1995. At http://www.saif.com/Safety_artc/aging.htm (accessed 5-28-98).

12. "Many Older Worker Myths Are Challenged by SHRM/AARP Survey," press release, Office of the Society for Human Resource Management, Alexandria, Va., May 15, 1998.

13. Jennifer J. Laabs, "What If They Don't Retire?" *Workforce,* December 1997, p. 59.

14. I discovered dozens of technologists with very similar stories in the course of conducting interviews for my book *Overcoming High-Tech Anxiety* (San Francisco: Jossey-Bass, 1999).

15. Craig A. Olson, "Who Receives Formal Firm-Sponsored Training in

the U.S.?" NCW Working Paper Series, University of California, Berkeley, 1996. At http://socs.berkeley.edu/-iir/ncw/papers/olson/page3.htm (accessed 12-21-98).

16. "Many Older Worker Myths Are Challenged by SHRM/AARP Survey," press release, office of the Society for Human Resource Management, Alexandria, Va., May 15, 1998.

17. Sherry Herchenroether, "Retain or Replace? Not So Rhetorical a Question," *Looking Ahead,* July 1991, pp. 39–43.

18. R. Roosevelt Thomas, Jr., *Beyond Race and Gender: Unleashing the Power of Your Total Work Force by Managing Diversity* (New York: Amacom, 1991), p. 130.

19. Sal Marano, "Of Age and Entrepreneurship," *Small Business News* (Pittsburgh edition), April 1998, pp. 10–11.

Chapter 6

1. Thomas A. Kochan, "The American Corporation as an Employer: Past, Present, and Future Possibilities," in *The American Corporation Today,* Carl Kaysen, ed. (New York: Oxford University Press, 1996), pp. 243–44.

2. Organisation for Economic Co-operation and Development, *Maintaining Prosperity in an Ageing Society* (Paris: OECD, 1998), p. 124.

3. Steve Rhodes, "At Work: What Full Employment Is Like," *Newsweek,* January 18, 1999, pp. 42–44.

4. The recommendations put forth are built on discussions with human resource experts, experience in developing and implementing change management programs, discussions with members of the Academy of Management, whose 1999 theme was the "change journey," and extensive investigations into the new flexible organization; for background on the development of that model, see John G. Sifonis and Beverly Goldberg, *Corporation on a Tightrope: Balancing Leadership, Governance, and Technology in an Age of Complexity* (New York: Oxford University Press, 1996).

5. David Leonhardt and Laura Cohn, "The Economy's Rising Tide," *Business Week,* April 26, 1999, pp. 30–31.

6. Author interview.

7. Greg Gillespie, "Compensation Trend: Not Just a Paycheck," *The Institute,* November 1996, available at http://www.institute.ieee.org/INST/nov96/comp.html (accessed 7-18-99).

8. Marc Adams, "The Stream of Labor Slows to a Trickle," *HR Magazine,* October 1998. At http://www.shrm.org/hrmagazine/articles/1098cov.htm (accessed 12-30-98).

9. Aon Consulting, *America@Work: A Focus on Benefits and Compensation* (Chicago: Aon Consulting, 1998), p. 9.

10. "Why Workers Don't Show Up," *Business Week,* November 16, 1998, p. 8.

11. Ken Sheets, "Over 50 and in Demand," *Kiplinger Personal Finance Magazine,* October 1997. At http://www.kiplinger.com/magazine/archives/1997/October/over50.html (accessed 12-30-98).

12. Michael Hickins, "Burning the Candle," *Management Review,* November 1998, p. 6.

13. Aon Consulting, *America@Work,* p. 9.

14. Pitney Bowes, Inc., "Pitney Bowes Study Finds Messaging Creates Greater Stress at Work," press release, Stamford, Conn., May 18, 1998.

15. From chapter 6 of Niccolò Machiavelli's *The Prince,* written in 1513.

16. I have recently helped two organizations formulate their new mission statements and the strategic and program goals that were considered an integral part of the mission: one was for the American Association of University Presses, the other for a troubled organization in the health care field.

Chapter 7

1. "Many Older Worker Myths Are Challenged by SHRM/AARP Survey," press release, office of the Society for Human Resource Management, Alexandria, Va., May 15, 1998.

Notes

2. Cheryl Comeau-Kirschner, "Human Capital Critical to Success," *Management Review,* November 1998, p. 9.

3. Marc Adams, "The Stream of Labor Slows to a Trickle," *HR Magazine,* October 1998, at http://www.shrm.org/hrmagazine/articles/1098cov.htm (accessed 12-30-98).

4. Charlotte Marmer Solomon, "Unlock the Potential of Older Workers," *Personnel Journal* 74, no. 10, October 1995, pp. 56–66.

5. Amy Dunkin, "Saying Adios to the Office," *Business Week,* October 12, 1998, pp. 152–56.

6. Jenny C. McCune, "The Future of Retirement," *Management Review,* April 1998, p. 15.

7. Susan A. MacManus, *Young v. Old: Generational Combat in the 21st Century* (Boulder, Colo.: Westview Press, 1996), p. 11.

8. James E. Challenger, "Wise Employers Plan 'Soft Landing' for Retirees," *Houston Business Journal,* January 6, 1997. At http://www.amcity.com/houston/stories/010697/editorial5.html (accessed 8-3-98).

9. Author interview.

10. "The Death of Corporate Loyalty," *Economist,* April 3, 1993, p. 63.

11. "Those Who Can, Teach," *Economist,* October 28, 1995, p. 79.

12. Louise Wah, "An Ounce of Prevention," *Management Review,* October 1998, p. 9.

13. Data from William M. Mercer, Inc., reported in "Up Front," *Business Week,* April 20, 1998, p. 8.

14. Sara E. Rix, "The Older Worker in a Graying America: Innovation, Choice, and Change," in *Life in an Older America,* Robert N. Butler, Lawrence K. Grossman, and Mia R. Oberlink, eds., a Century Foundation Book (New York: Century Foundation Press, 1999), p. 205.

15. AARP, *American Business and Older Workers: A Road Map to the 21st Century* (Washington, D.C.: AARP, 1995), p. 10.

16. Robert W. Thompson, "Study: HR Is Aware of Changes, But Is Slow to Respond," HR News Online, at www.shrm.org/hrnews/articles/061598c.htm (accessed 12-7-98).

17. Author interview.

18. Alexander P. Spence, *Biology of Human Aging,* 2d ed. (Englewood Cliffs, N.J.: Prentice-Hall, 1995), pp. 85–86.

Chapter 8

1. Edward A. Filene, *The Way Out: A Forecast of Coming Changes in American Business and Industry* (New York: Doubleday, Page & Company, 1926), pp. 30–31.
2. Christopher J. Farrell, "The Labor Pool Is Deeper Than It Looks," *Business Week*, November 24, 1997, p. 39.
3. Ibid.
4. Howard Gleckman, "A Rich Stew in the Melting Pot," *Business Week*, August 31, 1998, p. 76.
5. Peter G. Peterson, *Gray Dawn: How the Coming Age Wave Will Transform America—And the World* (New York: Times Books, 1999), pp. 135–47.
6. Michael Specter, "Population Implosion Worries a Graying Europe," *New York Times*, July 10, 1998, p. A6.
7. William H. Miller, "Forget 2000, Worry about 2010," *Industry Week*, October 6, 1997, p. 64.
8. Arne L. Kalleberg et al., "Nonstandard Work, Substandard Jobs: Flexible Work Arrangements in the United States," in *The Changing Nature of Work,* edited by Frank Ackerman et al. (Washington, D.C.: Island Press, 1998), p. 183.
9. Barbara B. Buchholz, "Back on the Job," *Chicago Tribune,* July 28, 1998, p. C1.
10. Nelson Lichtenstein, "American Trade Unions and the 'Labor Question': Past and Present," in *Does Labor Have a Future? The Report of The Century Foundation Task Force on the American Labor Movement* (New York: Century Foundation Press, forthcoming).
11. Stephen A. Herzenberg, John A. Alic, and Howard Wial, *New Rules for the New Economy: Employment and Opportunity in Postindustrial America,* a Twentieth Century Fund Book (Ithaca, N.Y.: Cornell University Press, 1998), pp. 164–65.
12. One of the best books on this subject is Charles Heckscher's *The New Unionism: Employee Involvement in the Changing Corporation.* A revised edition of this Twentieth Century Fund book was published by Cornell University Press in 1996.

13. Commonwealth Fund, *The Untapped Resource* (New York: Commonwealth Fund, 1993), pp. 36–37.
14. Author interview.
15. Editorial, *Arizona Republic,* May 17, 1998, p. 114.
16. June Fletcher, "Retirees Say No to Parents' Communities," *Wall Street Journal,* November 14, 1997, p. B14.
17. Filene, *The Way Out,* pp. 46–47.

Selected Bibliography

Aaron, Henry J., and Reischauer, Robert D. *Countdown to Reform: The Great Social Security Debate*. A Century Foundation Book. New York: Century Foundation Press, 1998.

Auerbach, James A. (ed.) *Through a Glass Darkly: Building a New Workplace for the 21st Century*. Washington, D.C.: National Policy Association, 1998.

Auerbach, James A., and Welch, Joyce C. (eds.) *Aging and Competition: Rebuilding the U.S. Workforce*. Washington, D.C.: National Planning Association, 1994.

Ball, Robert. *Straight Talk about Social Security*. A Twentieth Century Fund Report. New York: Twentieth Century Fund Press, 1998.

Barone, Michael. *Our Country: The Shaping of America from Roosevelt to Reagan*. New York: Free Press, 1990.

Bass, Scott. (ed.) *Older and Active: How Americans over 55 Are Contributing to Society*. New Haven, Conn.: Yale University Press, 1995.

Butler, Robert N., Grossman, Lawrence K., and Oberlink, Mia R. (eds.) *Life in an Older America*. A Century Foundation Book. New York: Century Foundation Press, 1999.

Capelli, Peter, et al. (eds.) *Change at Work*. New York: Oxford University Press, 1997.

211

Selected Bibliography

Cole, Thomas R. *The Journey of Life: A Cultural History of Aging in America.* Cambridge: Cambridge University Press, 1992.

Coleman, Penny. *Rosie the Riveter.* New York: Crown, 1995.

Commonwealth Fund. *The Untapped Resource: The Final Report of the Americans Over 55 at Work Program.* New York: Commonwealth Fund, 1993.

Costa, Dora L. *The Evolution of Retirement: An American Economic History, 1980–1990.* Chicago: University of Chicago Press, 1998.

Dychtwald, Ken. *Age Power: How the 21st Century Will Be Ruled by the New Old.* New York: Jeremy P. Tarcher/Putnam, 1999.

Dychtwald, Ken, and Flower, Joe. *Age Wave: How the Most Important Trend of Our Time Will Change Your Future.* New York: Bantam Books, 1990.

Erikson, Kai, and Vallas, Steven Peter. *The Nature of Work: Sociological Perspectives.* New Haven, Conn.: Yale University Press, 1990.

Esty, Katharine, Griffin, Richard, and Hirsch, Marcie Schorr. *Workplace Diversity.* Holbrook, Mass.: Adams Media Corporation, 1995.

Galbraith, James K. *Created Unequal: The Crisis in American Pay.* A Twentieth Century Fund Book. New York: Free Press, 1998.

Gluck, Sherna Berger. *Rosie the Riveter Revisited: Women, the War, and Social Change.* New York: Meridian, 1988.

Goldberg, Beverly, and Sifonis, John G. *Dynamic Planning: The Art of Managing Beyond Tomorrow.* New York: Oxford University Press, 1994.

Gordon, David M. *Fat and Mean: The Corporate Squeeze on Working Americans and the Myth of Managerial "Downsizing."* New York: Free Press, 1996.

Hamel, Gary, and Prahalad, C.K. *Competing for the Future.* Boston: Harvard Business School Press, 1994.

Handy, Charles. *The Age of Unreason.* Boston: Harvard Business School Press, 1991.

Harrison, Bennett. *Lean and Mean: The Changing Landscape of Corporate Power in the Age of Flexibility.* New York: Basic Books, 1994.

Heckscher, Charles. *White Collar Blues: Management Loyalties in an Age of Corporate Restructuring.* New York: Basic Books, 1995.

————. *The New Unionism: Employee Involvement in the Changing Corporation.* A Twentieth Century Fund Book. Ithaca, N.Y.: Cornell University Press, 1996.

Herzenberg, Stephen A., Alic, John A., and Wial, Howard. *New Rules for the New Economy: Employment and Opportunity in Postindustrial America.* A Twentieth Century Fund Book. Ithaca, N.Y.: Cornell University Press, 1998.

Jamieson, David, and O'Mara, Julie. *Managing Workforce 2000: Gaining the Diversity Advantage.* San Francisco: Jossey-Bass, 1991.

Judy, Richard W., and D'Amico, Carol. *Workforce 2020: Work and Workers in the 21st Century.* Indianapolis: Hudson Institute, 1997.

Katzenbach, Jon R., and Smith, Douglas K. *The Wisdom of Teams: Creating the High-Performance Organization.* Boston: Harvard Business School Press, 1993.

Kaysen, Carl. (ed.) *The American Corporation Today.* New York: Oxford University Press, 1996.

Kotlikoff, Laurence J. *Generational Accounting: Knowing Who Pays, and When, for What We Spend.* New York: Free Press, 1992.

Kuttner, Robert. *Everything for Sale.* A Twentieth Century Fund Book. New York: Knopf, 1996.

Leone, Richard C., and Anrig, Greg, Jr. (eds.) *Beyond the Basics: Social Security Reform.* A Century Foundation Book. New York: Century Foundation Press, 1999.

Levine, L. David. *Reinventing the Workplace: How Business and Employees Can Both Win.* Washington, D.C.: Brookings Institution Press, 1995.

Lozano, B. *The Invisible Workforce: Transforming American Business with Outside and Home-Based Workers.* New York: Free Press, 1989.

MacManus, Susan A. *Young v. Old: Generational Combat in the 21st Century.* Boulder, Colo.: Westview Press, 1996.

Mitchell, Olivia S. (ed.) *As the Workforce Ages: Costs, Benefits and Policy Challenges.* Ithaca, N.Y.: ILR Press, 1993.

Morris, Charles R. *The AARP: America's Most Powerful Lobby and the Clash of Generations.* New York: Times Books, 1996.

213

New York Times. *The Downsizing of America*. New York: Times Books, 1996.

Organisation for Economic Co-operation and Development. *Maintaining Prosperity in an Ageing Society*. Paris: OECD, 1998.

Osterman, Paul. (ed.) *Broken Ladders: Managerial Careers in the New Economy*. New York: Oxford University Press, 1996.

———. *Securing Prosperity: The American Labor Market: How It Has Changed and What to Do About It*. A Century Foundation Book. Princeton, N.J.: Princeton University Press, 1999.

Peterson, Peter G. *Will America Grow Up Before It Grows Old?* New York: Random House, 1996.

———. *Gray Dawn: How the Coming Age Wave Will Transform America—and the World*. New York: Times Books, 1999.

Rowden, Robert W. (ed.) *Workplace Learning: Debating Five Critical Questions of Theory and Practice*. San Francisco: Jossey-Bass, 1996.

Rudolph, Barbara. *Disconnected: How Six People from AT&T Discovered the New Meaning of Work in a Downsized Corporate America*. New York: Free Press, 1998.

Russell, Cheryl. *The Master Trend: How the Baby Boom Generation Is Remaking America*. New York: Plenum Press, 1993.

Russell, Louise B. *The Baby Boom Generation and the Economy*. Washington, D.C.: Brookings Institution Press, 1982.

Schein, Edgar H. *Organizational Culture and Leadership*. San Francisco: Jossey-Bass, 1985.

Schor, Juliet B. *The Overworked American: The Unexpected Decline of Leisure*. New York: Basic Books, 1991.

Sifonis, John G., and Goldberg, Beverly. *Corporation on a Tightrope: Balancing Leadership, Governance, and Technology in an Age of Complexity*. New York: Oxford University Press, 1996.

Silver, Don. *Baby Boomer Retirement: 65 Simple Ways to Protect Your Future*. Los Angeles: Adams-Hall, 1998.

Smith, Hendrick. *Rethinking America*. New York: Random House, 1995.

Spence, Alexander P. *Biology of Human Aging*. Englewood Cliffs, N.J.: Prentice-Hall, 1989.

Selected Bibliography

Spikes, W. Franklin. (ed.) *Workplace Learning.* San Francisco: Jossey-Bass, 1995.

Steuerle, C. Eugene, and Bakija, Jon. *Retooling Social Security for the 21st Century.* Washington, D.C.: Urban Institute Press, 1994.

Thau, Richard D., and Heflin, Jay S. (eds.) *Generations Apart: Xers vs. Boomers vs. the Elderly.* Amherst, N.Y.: Prometheus Books, 1997.

Thomas, R. Roosevelt, Jr. *Beyond Race and Gender: Unleashing the Power of Your Total Work Force by Managing Diversity.* New York: Amacom, 1991.

Torres-Gil, Fernando M. *The New Aging: Politics and Change in America.* New York: Auburn House, 1992.

Tulgan, Bruce. *Work This Way.* New York: Hyperion, 1998.

Wall, Ginita, and Collins, Victoria F. *Your Next Fifty Years: A Completely New Way to Look at How, When, and If You Should Retire.* New York: Henry Holt and Company, 1997.

Wolff, Edward N. *Top Heavy: The Increasing Inequality of Wealth in America and What Can Be Done About It.* A Twentieth Century Fund Report. New York: New Press, 1996.

Index

Index

Index

Commitment
  by corporation, 146
  to corporation, 42, 145, 162
  See also Social contract
Commonwealth Fund, 188
Communication and work 43–44, 130, 141–44, 146–47
Commuting, 20
Competing for the Future (Hamel and Prahalad), 66
Competing in a Global Economy, 114
Competition, 185
  international, 4, 41, 57, 59–60, 61, 66, 83, 185
Competitive advantage, 8, 66, 123, 150
Computer generation, 15, 21, 38
Consultants, xvi, 8, 115, 131, 150, 153–54
Consumers, xiii, 20–21, 49, 85
Contingent workers, 69, 74, 124, 148, 183
Contract workers, 5, 150, 153–54, 156, 175, 183
Core competencies, 66, 69
Corning Glass Company, 165
Corporate culture
  changing, 63, 108
  understanding, 118, 119, 120, 145, 153, 156
Corporate image, 10, 105, 135, 144, 145, 148
Corporate leadership, xiv, 9–10, 60, 125, 190–91
  role of, 105, 144, 151, 178
  See also Responsibility: of leaders
Corporate mission, 124, 130, 140, 145–46
Corporate strategy, 12, 48, 64, 76, 110, 124–25, 128–30, 190–91
  See also Downsizing; Restructuring of corporations
Corporate structure. *See* Organizational structure
Cost, 60, 63, 80, 118, 156

of labor, 64, 125, 151–52, 158, 188, 189
  See also Health care: costs; Salaries; Training of employees: costs
Costa, Dorothy, 86
Crawford, Robert J., 61
Creativity in work, 3, 10, 45, 55, 111–12, 113–14, 194

Days Inns Corporation, 132–33
Decision-making, 31, 66, 109–10, 128–30
  See also Retirement lifestyle: decisions
Defined benefit plans, 92
Defined contribution plans, 92–93, 118
Del Webb Corporation, 189
Demographic projections, 10, 11–12, 16, 19 fig. 1.1, 27, 35–36, 150
Demographic transition, xvi, 2, 15, 16–17, 18–19 fig. 1.1
  See also Birthrate; Population; Retirement age
Dependence ratio. *See* Employment-to-population ratio; Worker to pensioner ratio
DeWard, Donald, 155
Displaced workers, 11, 55, 73, 77, 108
  See also Downsizing; Layoffs
Diverse workforce, 104, 117–18, 124, 127–28, 150, 159, 175–76
Diversity programs, 118–20, 124, 127–28, 130, 146, 155, 175
Doran, Kevin, 174–75
Downsizing, 24, 119
  causes, 4–5, 66, 83
  effect on corporations, 3, 64, 73–74, 76, 81–82
  effect on workers, xv–xvi, 2, 11, 34, 41, 77, 109–10, 129
  implementing, 67–68, 77–80, 145, 168–69
  See also Displaced workers; Layoffs

221

Index

Index